PALACE HOTEL
GENERAL
R.K.

THE REAL BOOK ABOUT THE WILD WEST

THE REAL BOOK ABOUT

THE WILD WEST

BY

ADOLPH REGLI

Illustrated by Ted Shearer

EDITED BY HELEN HOKE

Garden City Books

GARDEN CITY, NEW YORK

BY ARRANGEMENT WITH FRANKLIN WATTS, INC.

1952
GARDEN CITY BOOKS

PRINTED IN THE UNITED STATES

To my sister
CAROLINE
who would have tamed the Wild West
but was born too late

ACKNOWLEDGMENTS

This is a book of many parts welded by mind and heart into the story of the Wild West's change and growth and thrilling romance. Into its writing have gone fact, history and anecdote from many sources. With deep gratitude the author acknowledges the help of such authorities and their works as Frederic L. Paxson's *History of the American Frontier* and *Last American Frontier*; Bernard A. De Voto's *Year of Decision, 1846*; Stanley Vestal's *Warpath and Council Fire* and *Short Grass Country*; Emerson Hough's *Story of the Cowboy*; Stuart N. Lake's *Wyatt Earp, Frontier Marshal*; George D. Hendricks' *Bad Men of the West*; Joseph L. French's *The Pioneer West* and Stewart Holbrook's writings in *The American Mercury*. Several magazines, notably *Holiday*, *Life*, *Esquire* and *Western Trailer Life*, also helped to round out the engrossing story.

ADOLPH REGLI

Contents

CHAPTER 1

What Made the West Wild

THE West has always challenged strong and daring spirits, ever since the first settlers came to American shores. From the nation's beginning the West has been a magic and romantic word, tempting brave people to search its vast mysteries for riches and new homes. Its lure has never weakened; the pioneer spirit moves strongly in the West of today.

It is a region that has meant different things to different people at different times. The forests and mountains of New York, Pennsylvania and West Virginia made up the West of the early colonists along the Atlantic coast. Later another West came into being—the rich farm lands of Ohio, Kentucky, Indiana, Illinois and Wisconsin.

For the young United States the Mississippi River was the frontier, beyond which lay . . . what? Few settlers knew or cared. Why worry about the vague plains and mountains so far off when there were millions of acres still lying idle east of the Mississippi?

There were people of the Old World, however, who took a lively interest in the rugged land of Indians and wild animals. While the American colonies were struggling to live, England and France sent explorers into the wilderness. A few came down from Hudson Bay in Canada—others crossed the Great Lakes and then paddled up long rivers and marched over the prairies.

After the explorers came the traders and fur hunters. They made friends of the Indians and bought beaver, otter and marten skins to send to Europe by the bale. To the fur companies this new West offered great wealth.

Spain also sent scouts into the American wilderness. Her soldiers came northward from Mexico, across the dry plains and into the mountains, seizing all they saw for their king. By 1800 western America was being taken over by Europeans.

Spanish territory stretched from Texas to California. The British claimed what is now Oregon and Washington, the Pacific Northwest. The French held a great triangle of land extending north and south from New Orleans to Duluth, Minnesota, and westward to the Rocky Mountains. This entire area bore the name Louisiana.

The Mississippi River had become the chief highway to New Orleans. Down it floated barges, rafts and keelboats with produce from the Ohio Valley farms. With the French holding the western bank there was danger of Americans losing the free use of the river. It appeared, too, that the Mississippi would

Boats of all kinds floated down the Mississippi

become the western border of the United States.

To prevent this, the American government in 1803 bought Louisiana from France. For fifteen million dollars it gained almost a million square miles of plains and mountains. What else the region contained few persons had more than the foggiest idea.

To explore this great unknown, President Thomas

Jefferson sent out a party under Meriwether Lewis and William Clark. The group spent two years traveling by river boat, horses and canoes from St. Louis to the Pacific Coast and back.

Besides visiting Indian tribes never before seen by white men, Lewis and Clark brought back a report of snow-capped mountains, surging rivers and sweeping plains. It was a land of beauty, rich in furs, boundless in hidden wealth. The Louisiana Purchase, they proved, was one of America's best bargains.

News that fur-bearing animals abounded in the mountains started the first westward drive of bold men from the American border to join a handful of trappers already there. Fur was the gold of that period —and here was an almost untouched source. Soon groups of traders traveled up the Missouri River to set up trading posts where they could barter with the Indians for beaver pelts.

With the traders went scores of free trappers, daring and carefree soldiers of fortune who worked alone to snare the wily beaver. They became known as the mountain men of the early wild West.

The free trapper was in a class apart from the employees of British and French fur companies. The hired men worked under strict company bosses for wages, while the Americans roamed where they willed, fought their own fights and pocketed what they earned.

After a winter's trapping the mountain men packed their furs to trading posts on the Platte or Arkansas rivers, or farther south to the Mexican settlements of Taos and Santa Fe. At such rendezvous they sold their furs and spent a week in wild fun. Then broke and tired of seeing people, they set out to spend another year in their lonely wanderings.

The fur trade led to another business that was to give the West a new mode of travel. Traders venturing out to Santa Fe found there a demand for tools, cloth, utensils and trinkets made in the East. These goods were paid for in furs, articles of silver and Mexican dollars.

The loads pack animals could carry were limited. Another means was needed for hauling all the material wanted by the Santa Fe buyers. That method was found in the freight wagon—drawn by mules or oxen.

Loaded with tons of merchandise the heavy wagons set out from Independence, a small city on the big bend of the Missouri River. Six or eight wagons, sometimes more, formed a train to cross eight hundred miles of grassland, dry plains and mountains. Their route became known as the Santa Fe Trail.

Meantime, many people in the East were tiring of their poor land, lack of markets for their crops or low factory wages. They packed their household goods into wagons and started for the Middle West.

Soon Ohio, Indiana and Illinois became too crowded for the earliest settlers and they pushed across the Mississippi to take up homesteads and form a new farm frontier.

In 1842 John C. Frémont began his explorations of the Far West and became known as the Pathfinder. His reports started a great tide of people into Oregon. Thousands sought to escape the hard times back East by making the long and difficult wagon journey over the Oregon Trail.

For another twenty-five years the lurching covered wagon was to compete with Indians and buffalo for the right of way across the plains.

This stirring of the West came at a time when disputes reached a head along the Rio Grande. Texas, now the home of many Americans from the South, broke away from Mexico and became a part of the United States. In 1846, the United States and Mexico went to war, a short war that added New Mexico, Arizona and California to American territory. At last the young republic stretched from coast to coast, although most of it was still wild and savage. The war with Mexico had brought an army into the West and started the tragic clashes with the Plains Indians.

Hardly had the United States whipped Mexico when the discovery of gold in California set the nation wild with new excitement. Everyone, it appeared, wanted to rush to the Pacific Coast and dig a quick fortune from the streams around Sutter's Fort.

The finding of gold—perhaps more than any one other thing—gave direction of a sort to the settling of the West!

The movement to California became a stampede. Gentlemen and criminals, farmers and gamblers, clerks and laborers dropped everything to climb into covered wagons and begin the two-thousand-mile drive from the Missouri River to the gold fields. The news spread around the world—and before long adventurers by the boatload arrived at San Francisco to join in the mad rush.

Once in the camps the miners found life severe, even brutal. They lived in leaky tents or drafty shacks. Food was scarce and costly. There was no police force, no law or justice except that forced upon the camps by honest men. Death was the usual punishment for thieves and murderers.

The Indian tribes watched the growing numbers of emigrant and freight wagons with rising anger. In trust and good faith they had given up land along the farm frontier in exchange for hunting grounds farther west. The whites had promised not to invade their distant homes.

But the treaties were being broken by the hordes of white men spreading across the plains. Wherever they went the buffalo and other game began to disappear. To the tribes on the plains the buffalo meant food, shelter and clothing. If they vanished, the Indians would perish.

With arrows, tomahawks, lances and rifles—the only weapons they could make the invaders understand—the warriors struck back, killing isolated families and emigrant parties.

Army troops rushed out from Fort Leavenworth to punish the attackers. To answer the westerners' appeals for protection, the Army built more forts along the Platte and Missouri rivers and in the Powder River country of Wyoming. Huge freight wagons lumbered back and forth with supplies for the soldiers.

The angry Indians fought back savagely. As they found themselves being crowded off their hunting grounds they took to the warpath. The bloodiest uprising occurred in Minnesota where the Sioux killed several hundred settlers.

The West braced itself for a war to the finish.

New gold discoveries started fresh stampedes to the Pikes Peak district of Colorado and to Nevada, Idaho and Montana. They came after a period of hard times in the East when banks failed and jobs were scarce. The East poured thousands of its idle young men into the growing West, many of them drawn by promises of excitement and adventure.

Despite the lawlessness in the gold fields and warfare against the Indians, the West went on with its more peaceful business. Stagecoach lines began to operate between St. Louis and San Francisco, from Fort Leavenworth to Denver and Salt Lake City.

To speed the mail from Missouri to California, which took twenty-five days by coach, a pony express was started. Young riders, a few only fifteen and sixteen years old, rode swift horses in relays across two thousand miles of plain, desert and mountain passes to deliver express and mail in ten days between St. Joseph and San Francisco. The pony express served faithfully until the telegraph spanned the nation and ended its usefulness.

By then a railroad had crossed the Mississippi and reached out into Kansas. Besides giving homesteaders a means of shipping their crops to eastern markets, the railway put life into the cattle business.

Texas was full of longhorn cattle—worth little except for their hides. Thousands ran wild on the plains, fair game for any rancher willing to hire a crew of cowboys to round them up. The cost was hardly worth the bother for the cattlemen had no way of getting the beef to slaughterhouses in Kansas City and Chicago.

But once a railroad line came within a few hundred miles of the Texas ranges, the longhorns became valuable. Cattlemen began to trail large herds overland to the shipping pens. Crews of cowhands rode beside two or three thousand head of steers, guarding them against thieves, Indians and storms.

Cattle by the hundreds of thousands moved up the

trails from Texas, across Indian Territory (now Oklahoma) and into Kansas. Texas ranchers grew rich as the demand for beef increased.

Their success encouraged cattle-rustling gangs—dishonest men who raided herds, changed the brands and sold the steers as their own. In a lawless land the injured rancher made his own law. A captured rustler usually paid for his crime by death at the end of a cowboy's rope.

Along the railroad, cow towns like Abilene and Dodge City took root to serve the Texas herders. When they reached the end of the long trail, the wild and carefree cowhands had money to spend—and they played and gambled until it was gone. With six-shooters at their sides, they were ready for fun or a fight—whichever came their way.

Wherever there was money and excitement, a crowd of tough and ruthless men was certain to gather. The bitterness left by the Civil War often flared into violence when Texans and Yankees met. Outlaws, gunmen and criminals challenged the sheriffs and United States marshals.

For many years the nation had looked forward to a railroad that would span the continent. The Civil War had interfered, but when it was over work on a railroad right of way from Council Bluffs, Iowa, to Sacramento, California, started in the late 1860's.

Builders started at both the eastern and western

ends of the line, working toward each other. Crews of graders, rail layers and bridge gangs raced to see which could put down the most miles of track. They met at Promontory Point in Utah in 1869. This was the swiftest and most important step in the exciting growth of the West.

The railroad had far-reaching effects on western life and business. No longer was it necessary to haul freight hundreds of miles in slow-moving wagons. The prairie schooner of the first settlers all but vanished. Farm families seeking cheap and better land—and others tired of city life—boarded trains by the thousands and rode west in comfort to take up homesteads. They were joined by a mass of Europeans who hoped to find freedom in America, land on which to build homes and a better life.

As the settlers fenced in the prairies and plains that had been the cattlemen's open range, the cow country retreated to the high plateaus and mountain districts. Wheat and corn replaced the pasture lands from Texas to Montana.

In 1874 the discovery of gold in the Black Hills of South Dakota started the Plains Indians' last fight for survival. The Black Hills and other lands to the west belonged to the Sioux and Cheyenne tribes—theirs by treaty with the United States. The government had agreed to keep the whites out of the last great hunting grounds of Sitting Bull and Crazy Horse's people.

But the magic word *gold* made it impossible to keep that promise. Against government orders, gold hunters stampeded to Custer Creek and Deadwood Gulch, fighting off the red men who tried to drive them out.

To protect the miners the Army sent three columns of troops into the area. Sioux and Cheyenne warriors, joining in the greatest band of fighting Indians ever seen in the West, met the challenge.

They turned back one army column and massacred General George Custer and much of his Seventh Cavalry on the Little Big Horn River in Montana. But in doing so, the last great nations of red men lost their homes, most of their horses and even their lives. In despair the remaining Indians were herded into reservations to live as wards of the national government.

Except for scattered and hopeless outbreaks the American Indians were crushed and the West was free to make of itself what it wished.

That wish has been realized in the beautiful land of bounty we know the West to be today. Its farms and ranches, its mines, forests, cattle, orchards, railroads, air lines, water power, oil and widespread industries are fruits of the dreams and hopes of the pioneers. The covered wagons carried those dreams and hopes over rough and rocky trails. Young spirits of more recent days have built bigger and better, but never more boldly.

CHAPTER 2

Mountain Men

A YOUNG fur trapper, traveling afoot and alone in the high Rockies, stopped suddenly to stare ahead in awe. He had seen many strange things on his journeys through the mountains but never a sight to compare with this.

The entire hillside before him was a terrace of colors, step upon step of yellow, orange and rusty browns. Steam arose from water that boiled inside the crusted bowls. The winter's first snow was upon the ground but winter's deepest drifts would never put out that fire on the smoking slope.

"Now what do you reckon put a flint to *that* kettle of brew?" the trapper muttered aloud. For long minutes he stood gazing in wonder, but found no answer.

He moved on for several days amid other fantastic sights—geysers that spouted vapor above the treetops, springs of clear boiling water, basins full of bubbling mud, cones and mounds and other formations colored brightly by streams flowing from them. He saw galloping rivers, massive waterfalls, deep gorges and a great lake crowded together on this high plateau of smoke pots and hot springs.

"Nary a sane man will believe me," the trapper mumbled, "when I tell them what these doubting eyes have seen. And I can't blame them if they say my tongue is crooked."

This lone traveler was John Colter, the first white man to visit that show place of nature which would someday be known as Wyoming's Yellowstone Park. It was late in 1807, the year after Lewis and Clark had returned from their journey to the Pacific Coast.

John Colter had shared the dangers and hardships with these explorers, winning their respect for his daring and trust. On the way home he expressed a wish to remain behind to become a fur trapper. Lewis and Clark released him with their blessings.

About that time another trapper named Manuel Lisa was building a trading post at the mouth of the Big Horn River. Lisa hired Colter to visit distant Crow and other Indian tribes to win their trade. It was on this mission, through a region unknown to white men, that Colter crossed the Yellowstone district.

The next spring Colter and a companion, John Potts, left with a party of friendly Crow and Flathead Indians to trap beaver at the Three Forks of the Missouri River, in present-day Montana. This was dangerous country for them because the Blackfoot tribe guarded it jealously.

Colter and his party avoided their enemy for a time but finally the Blackfeet cornered them. In a savage battle, John Potts was slain, along with several Crows and Flatheads.

As his peril increased, John Colter searched wildly for a means of escape. He would have to depend upon his wits and his legs once he broke out of the Blackfoot ambush.

Just then an arrow plowed through his arm and into his shoulder. It was a serious wound, he knew. Now escape seemed hopeless.

He jerked the arrow from his body and crept toward a screen of brush that led into a gorge. If he could reach it he had a chance to get away from the battleground. He snaked his way along, a foot at a time.

Another yard and he would— A sudden yell chilled him. An alert Blackfoot had seen Colter's slight movement. In an instant the pack was after him. Colter leaped to his feet and started to run.

Slipping and falling, Colter reached the bottom of the gorge. He lost his rifle during the tumble but dared not stop to search for it. Zigzagging to keep trees between himself and his pursuers, he sped along the bank of a creek as the howling Blackfeet pressed upon him.

Colter had no doubt of his ability to outrun the Blackfeet. He was a frontiersman of the Daniel Boone type, made strong and wiry by the privations and rugged life he lived. But because of his wound, the enemy now had the advantage. Colter knew that when his injury began to drain his strength he would be overtaken. But until the last ounce of strength left him he would race on grimly for his life.

Colter broke out of the gorge and picking his path to obtain all the protection possible from the rough ground, he held his lead just out of arrow range. He wanted to save all the energy he could.

Colter lost track of time and distance. His wound felt like a log on his back and his arm burned as though touched by a torch. His legs began to weaken and grow weary. How much longer could he go on?

A blur of gray water wavered in front of him. He staggered once and recovered his balance by pure will. An arrow whizzed past his head and he heard the pack closing upon him. A howl of triumph spurred him to a last burst of power.

He found himself on a high bank of a broad river. Without slackening his speed he leaped into the stream and made no immediate effort to regain the surface.

Finally he thrust his head above the water and gasped to fill his lungs. The Indians spied him and drove several arrows into the river, missing him narrowly. Colter let himself drop from sight and started swimming under the surface.

Whenever forced to the surface for air he saw the Blackfeet keeping pace along the riverbank. Their arrows were falling wider—now that he had gained midstream.

Just as hope began to build up in him, Colter saw three of the Blackfeet dive into the river and swim toward him. They had no thought of giving up the chase.

Then a sharp curve in the river carried him from the Indians' sight. He noted an overhanging bank of the stream beyond which lay a shallow backwash filled with reeds. If he could reach it. . . .

He pulled out of the river's grip to reach the shoal water, and pushed himself among the reeds, breaking off a hollow stem as he did so. He placed it into his mouth and lay back among the rushes. When the water covered him again, he breathed through the tube.

He held himself still for many minutes. He could neither see nor hear; he could only worry over how long the Blackfeet would search for him.

Cautiously, he raised his head until an ear was out of the water. He heard the muffled sound of feet close by, then the puzzled grunts of the searchers. The Blackfeet were still around. Colter lowered his head slowly, thankful that the reeds hid him so well.

After an agony of waiting it grew dark. He raised himself warily and listened for many minutes for the dreaded sounds. He heard nothing.

So numbed that he could hardly lift his legs, he

crawled from the water and rested on the riverbank. Then gazing at the night sky to find the North Star as his guide, he set out for Manuel Lisa's trading post on the Big Horn River. A few days later he stumbled into the stockade, gaunt and half starved.

John Colter's flight from the Blackfeet was only one of many narrow escapes he experienced while a trapper. Danger held a charm for him and he returned again and again to risk death among the Blackfeet.

Few mountain men saw anything heroic in their meeting and conquering of natural enemies—hostile Indians, wild animals and evil weather. They chose to live in a wilderness that called for strength, bravery and skill in their trade. For the most part, they were silent men whose deeds are lost in the unwritten history of the West.

There are names like Christopher "Kit" Carson, James Bridger, Thomas Fitzpatrick, the four Bent brothers, the five Sublettes, William Williams, Ceran St. Vrain and William Becknell that rank at the top for their outstanding gifts to the West. As traders, guides, scouts, Indian agents, fighters—or whatever their talents—they were the explorers who blazed the trails for others coming after them.

A few of the mountain men were known for rare feats of endurance—men like James Beckwourth, who claimed he saved his scalp by outrunning Blackfeet pursuers in a ninety-five-mile foot race. Or a man like

John Glass, who crawled eighty miles to camp after killing a bear that had torn strips of flesh from his chest, arms and legs, clawed his face horribly and pulled his scalp down over his eyes.

All knew danger and adventure—their reason for being mountain men. The profit from a pack of beaver pelts was a mere by-product.

Freedom from the curbs of civilized life meant more to them than kingdoms and palaces. They were mountain men, at home only among their own.

CHAPTER 3

The Trail to Santa Fe

HALF a dozen pack mules loaded with bolts of cloth, shawls and light articles of hardware and cutlery straggled along the upper waters of the Arkansas River in Colorado. William Becknell, a young trader and explorer, prodded his slow-paced animals over the hot, rocky trail.

It was the year of 1821 and Becknell wanted to reach Santa Fe as quickly as possible. Important news had come from the South a few weeks earlier. Mexico had revolted and shaken off Spanish rule—now perhaps American traders would be welcomed instead of being thrown into prison or chased back north.

Come what may, Becknell intended to be the first into Santa Fe. Turning south from the Arkansas River he passed through Taos, an old meeting place of mountain fur trappers, and reached his goal.

To Becknell's delight, his welcome was warm indeed. The Mexican traders snapped up everything he had to sell at prices that made his eyes bulge. Never before had his profits been so large. At once he made up his mind to come back the next year, but with a larger stock of goods.

It was late autumn when he returned to his starting place on the Missouri River. He spent the winter months getting ready for another journey to Santa Fe. This time he would load his freight into wagons and hire teamsters to drive his mules. He advertised in a newspaper and soon had a company of men signed up.

Having room to haul several tons of freight, he loaded his wagons with cotton and woolen goods, hardware, silk shawls, looking glasses and similar articles shipped to him from the East. When the grass that spring was long enough to feed his livestock Becknell set out for Santa Fe.

Instead of following the old route that swung far north into Colorado, he led his train away from the Arkansas at a point where Dodge City, Kansas, now stands, crossed to the Cimarron, followed the south fork of that stream to the forks of the Canadian River, went over a mountain pass and thus reached Santa Fe. It was a journey of eight hundred miles.

The year was hot and dry and the men and animals suffered greatly from dust and thirst, yet Becknell found that the effort paid off handsomely. Again he sold all his goods and took home bales of furs, Spanish dollars and bars of silver and gold.

With his first wagon caravan across the plains and mountains, he had traced a new route to the Southwest, a road that would become famous as the Santa Fe Trail. So successful had he been, in fact, that other traders gave up their pack mules for freight wagons.

At first the Indians were more of a nuisance than a danger because they merely flocked around the freighters' camps to beg and steal. But when the visiting tribesmen were chased off they became hostile, their attacks upon the trains creating a more serious threat.

In 1825 the United States government made a treaty with the Osage and Kansa tribes in which the Indians agreed to let the traders cross the plains in peace. At the same time, the government spent thirty thousand dollars to survey and mark the trail from the Missouri River to the United States-Mexican border on the Arkansas River.

Despite the treaty with the Indians it soon became clear that the Santa Fe traders would need army protection against Comanche and Kiowa war parties.

In 1827 the War Department built a post on the Missouri River just above the Kansas and called it Fort Leavenworth. Troops of soldiers went out from Leavenworth to escort wagon trains to the Arkansas River, the limits of United States territory.

By now there were enough traders going to Santa Fe to call for a system of travel. The wagons would leave the river towns singly or in small groups and head for Council Grove, one hundred and fifty miles to the west. There, beside the Neosho River in a heavily timbered spot, a great camp of freighters grew.

The grassy meadows around the camp were filled with oxen and mules grazing before their start across the dry plains. Dozens of huge Conestoga and Pittsburg wagons, loaded with three to five thousand pounds of freight each, stopped to tighten iron tires and waterproof canvas tops.

The teamsters and bullwhackers—the men who drove the eight to twelve mules or oxen that pulled each wagon—sat around campfires eating huge meals of meat, beans and biscuits and drinking coffee. Their laughter and shouts rang through the grove as they joked and told stories. Council Grove offered the last chance to relax before the hard journey over the prairie began.

Traders often spent several days at the grove while waiting for an escort of soldiers. If twenty-five or more wagons were ready to leave, the owners elected a captain to boss the company—and they began the long westward march without protection. Such a large force was usually safe from Indian raiders.

Once on the trail, the train moved with the order of an army column. The captain rode ahead on horseback to scout the trail and look for hostile warriors. Where the trail was wide the wagons formed parallel columns; more often they were strung out in one long line.

West of Council Grove the treeless prairie began. Water was usually scarce, grass often hard to find—while dust rose in great clouds to stifle men and animals alike. Each day the wagons shifted places—the leader on today's drive dropping to the rear tomorrow and the others moving up one position. Thus each driver took the worst of the dust and heat in his turn.

Camps were made twice daily, at noon and at night. Each time the wagons were drawn into a circle, or corral, with the tongue of one overlapping the vehicle ahead. An opening, about a wagon's length in size, was left through which the oxen could be driven after they had been watered and fed. The corral not only kept the animals penned in at night but served as protection for the men in case of an Indian attack.

The trains covered from twelve to fifteen miles a day. On its western half the trail grew more rough and difficult. River crossings, steep grades, deep sand and waterless stretches called for toughness of body and spirit. Sometimes, after six to eight weeks on the road, the stock was scarcely able to stand.

The arrival at Santa Fe called for a celebration. Just before reaching town the freighters would trim their hair and whiskers, bathe and wash their clothes and spruce up generally. The chance to enjoy the pleasures of Santa Fe was worth the hardship to get there.

After spending a week or ten days trading and resting up, the wagon train headed for home, taking back furs, money and goods made by skilled Mexican workmen. Because a round trip took five or six months, traders planned but one journey a year.

During the 1830's Independence, Missouri, became the chief starting point of the Santa Fe traders and grew to be a rough and lively frontier town.

Sprinkled among the rough and bearded veterans of the trail were young men, some in their early teens. One such was seventeen-year-old Christopher Carson, the Kit Carson who started his career as trapper, guide and soldier by working his way west as a "cavvy boy" —a horse herder with a wagon train.

The trail became the testing ground for many others of Carson's age and spirit. Those who did a man's work and faced danger with coolness and daring found a welcome among the lusty crews.

Until 1843 the freight trains plodding out to Santa Fe made up the only regular wagon travel across the plains. Suddenly the nation's attention shifted in another direction—the Northwest. It resulted from John Frémont's report of rich farm land, great forests and mighty streams that he found while exploring the Oregon country.

The East was ready to heed this call to a new frontier. Farmers were being driven from their poor land by lack of markets for their meager crops. Factory hands were paid little for their long hours of work. People were leaving Europe to find new homes in America. Oregon promised free land, new opportunity, a better life for everyone. Thousands more packed up and started west.

CHAPTER 4

The Rush to Oregon

IN THE early spring, families of farmers, laborers, blacksmiths, storekeepers and clerks, teachers, lawyers, ministers—all sorts of homeseekers—began gathering in the river towns around Fort Leavenworth.

Many came by boat up the Missouri River, while others drove overland in whatever wagons and carriages they owned. At the edge of the plains they made ready for the eighteen-hundred-mile journey on the prairie and mountain road known as the Oregon Trail.

Often a family's last dollar went for a wagon, livestock and food. Oxen were needed to haul the heavy load, a cow or two went along to provide milk—while a horse carried the head of the family.

Young bachelors, itching for adventure and new sights, came west without funds, hoping to work their passage by driving a team and serving as handy men for travelers of means.

The young people were the most eager and excited. In breathless groups, boys and girls scurried about to see everything possible. They became lost and worried their parents. With newly made friends they played tag, run sheep run and hopscotch. At meal-

The children sat about the campfire

time they sat upon the ground about a campfire, holding plates in their laps. At night they slept inside the wagons if there was room—otherwise they spread blankets outdoors.

Most of these people were greenhorns who knew

nothing of the trail that would take them along the Platte River through Nebraska, then into Wyoming and across the high plains to the distant mountains. Few gave much thought to the dangers and hardships they would face.

Before setting out in groups—varying from a score to several hundred wagons—each party elected a captain, a secretary, a treasurer and judges. They had the best intentions of keeping law and order among themselves.

But no sooner had a train left the Missouri border than disputes and strife began. Usually the company broke up, one bunch pushing ahead, others straggling to the right or left. All order and system vanished.

As the trail became rougher, accidents plagued the travelers. Wagon tongues snapped, wheels crumpled, rigs overturned on steep slopes and at river fords. Swamps, quicksand and high water were common hazards. Rain at night meant soaked blankets and a cold breakfast.

By day the hot sun broiled the toiling travelers. Nearly everyone caught colds—dysentery struck down hundreds, while few escaped red and swollen eyes from the dust, wind and sun. Animals strayed and their owners wasted hours chasing them. Travel became painfully slow.

Sometimes the grass all but vanished. Prized pieces of furniture, stoves and utensils had to be thrown away because the gaunt oxen could no longer pull the heavy loads. Always fear rode with them—fear of accident, sickness and Indians, of being stranded in the vast emptiness.

Through it all, the young people took a lively interest in the changing scene. Released from the lurching wagons when they stopped to camp, the boys and girls ran about and shouted in sheer joy until parents could stand the racket no longer and hushed them.

It was not all play for the children. Some gathered wood or dry buffalo chips for campfires. Others tended the animals while they grazed. Girls helped their mothers cook, bake and sew; boys worked with their fathers repairing broken wagon parts. There were few idle moments for anyone. Children were expected at an early age to take a hand in all family duties.

In the evenings groups gathered to talk over the day's events, to sing together, perhaps to listen to a sermon. Prayers for safety and guidance were spoken. A violin or harmonica player was hailed with delight at campfire meetings.

Now and then a wagon train caught a distant view of several Indian horsemen watching its passing. Children were both thrilled and frightened by the red men. Such a sight always sent a shiver through the travelers, especially after warnings drifted back from parties far ahead to be on the lookout. The tribesmen were dangerous along the North Platte River.

It had not always been so. The first white men who entered the West found most Indians friendly and helpful. The mountain men had many partners among the tribes. It was after the whites became serious rivals for the game, furs and the land itself that the red men became alarmed. Battles took place when they could not drive out the white men otherwise.

Life for the Indians was simple for they made everything they needed. Free to move about as they wished, they followed the buffalo herds, held their tribal dances and worshiped the Great Spirit. Horses were their only wealth and they prized them. In winter they gathered in villages made snug against storms and ate meat they had cured during their summer hunts.

Indian children were cared for tenderly and their days were happy and busy. As soon as they could shoot a bow and arrow, the boys practiced to become skillful hunters. They spent hours on ponies and became expert riders. The girls learned how to dress game, cook and sew. They married when quite young and joined the other squaws in doing all the camp work.

When white traders appeared among them the Indians trapped animals and sold their skins for beads, looking glasses and other trinkets. But they wanted little more than that from the whites. Most of all, they wished to be left alone.

Times changed after wagon trains began moving out to Santa Fe and to Oregon. The fear with which the Indians at first watched their coming soon turned to anger. For wherever the white men made their roads the buffalo and other game disappeared. Food was harder to find.

The white men were not keeping their promise to stay off the plains. The Indians began to attack wagon trains, killing teamsters and burning their goods.

Although the Army built forts along the Santa Fe and Oregon trails to protect the whites, the soldiers were too few to guard all of the long, lonely routes. Every wagon train had to be ready to make its own fight should a war party of braves appear suddenly.

Fear of such raids grew day by day as the travelers moved farther out upon the plains. Where would the painted and yelling warriors strike next without warning? Who would be the victims of their arrows and tomahawks tomorrow—or the next day?

CHAPTER 5

Indian Attack

THIRTY-SIX oxen, dark with sweat, strained to draw six covered wagons up a sandy slope in central Wyoming. At the top of the long grade the trail to Oregon angled right. It curled away from a bare mesa, one of the wartlike mounds of rock that dotted the high western plains.

Tired, hot and bored to silence, a woman and three small children rode in the first wagon. A boy of fourteen years drove the three yoke of oxen.

A little girl stirred herself from the wagon floor and tugged at her mother's dress. "Mama, I'm thirsty. I want another drink."

"Hush, dear," the mother said. "You must wait until we make camp. Our water is almost gone, you know. We were not able to fill our kegs this morning as we had hoped to."

"But I'm thirsty," the child said.

"I know, dear. We all are. But we must be brave and wait until we cross another creek. Then we will have all we want."

The train captain rode well ahead of the wagons—on the alert for hostile Crow Indians. He glanced back once or twice to make sure that none of his party was lagging. There were thirty-two men, women and children in the train—depending upon him for safety.

A nagging doubt refused to be turned aside. Had he and the others been wise in breaking away from the larger train that started from Missouri nearly three months before? The slow pace had irked them. They were impatient to reach Oregon and had gone on ahead.

Now, however, danger was closing about them. Two days earlier they had come upon the black ruins of burned wagons and several scalped bodies. They stopped only long enough to bury the victims. The next day smoke signals arose in the mountains to the west. And that very morning the captain had seen pony tracks across the trail. The drivers carried rifles in the crooks of their elbows as they toiled beside the oxen.

The captain was watching the mesa at the moment a Crow war party swept from behind it. Whipping their ponies, a score of warriors dashed straight toward the wagon train.

"Indians! Indians!" the captain shouted, swinging his horse around. "Corral the wagons. Hurry! Turn your wagons!"

Before the captain reached the column the drivers had started to draw the train into a tight circle. Once a corral was thus formed, the travelers would find shelter behind the wagons from the Indians' arrows and lances.

The oxen were slow and the time short. The last wagon was not yet in place before most of the men and older boys threw themselves into position to meet the attack. Women and children cowered behind the thin canvas coverings.

Their bodies streaked with red-and-yellow paint and their faces a hideous green, the Crows tore down upon the party, yelling like fiends. When they were a dozen yards away they sent arrows ripping through the wagon tops. Lances banged against sideboards or found targets in soft flesh.

The white men's rifles began to crack. Two howling horsemen toppled from their mounts, rolled crazily on the earth and lay still just outside the corral. The others raced past, spun around and sped back.

The second charge created wild confusion inside the corral. Still hitched to their wagons the oxen began to plunge and bellow, several breaking away and escaping. Half of the Indians raced after the animals, firing arrows into them.

Then they grouped for another charge on the train. But now the men inside the corral had steadied their nerves—and their second blast of gunfire turned aside the rushing braves.

The Crows were not discouraged, however. Again and again they rode close to whip arrows at the de-

A boy seized a rifle and fired into the face of an attacking Indian

fenders. Before long only a dozen men and boys were able to keep firing at the Indians.

Several women, who had overcome their fright, left the wagons to reload rifles for their husbands and to care for the wounded. A boy of twelve years slipped away from his mother, seized a rifle from an injured man and fired into the green face of a howling Indian trying to force his pony into the corral. The warrior's red-and-yellow-striped body fell across a wagon tongue and never moved again.

During a lull in the battle the captain moved among his people to keep up their courage. Two of the party were dead and four wounded, one a young boy. Eight Indians had been put out of the fight but they still outnumbered the fighting whites. Unless help came his group would be wiped out, the captain knew.

With the coming of darkness the Indians withdrew to the mesa but kept the travelers in their sight. The wagon party ate a cold supper. The youngest children whimpered for water but the last cupfuls went to the wounded men. No one in the corral slept that night. Everyone knew the ordeal would begin again the next morning.

At daybreak the Crows swooped upon the train in a howling rush. Their dead buried and defenses built up, the travelers fought back stubbornly. Unable to take the corral by storm, the Indians resumed their circling attack.

Reddened eyes scanned the back trail, looking for a film of dust that would herald the coming of another wagon train. Unless one appeared that day it would be too late.

Their thirst now a constant agony, the little band

could only hope and wait. The Crows grew more cautious but gave no sign of ending the siege. They had the hot sun, hunger and thirst on their side to wear down their victims.

Noon passed. The Indians gathered out of rifle range to rest their ponies. Inside the corral the train captain sat down wearily, his back against a wheel.

His eldest daughter, a girl of eleven, climbed to the wagon seat to gaze across the sandy plain. The captain said, "Get down, child. Do not show yourself to the Indians. It will tempt them to strike again."

"But, Father, perhaps I will see—"

"Get down, child. There is nothing to see."

"Oh, but there is," the girl said excitedly. "There . . . that little cloud of dust."

The captain sprang to his feet. For a minute, he gazed eastward, in the direction the girl was pointing. Was it . . . could it be? He and the others had prayed without ceasing for rescue. Their only hope was the arrival of another wagon train.

"Do you think it is one, Father?" the girl asked anxiously.

"I . . . I'm not sure yet, child. Say nothing to the others. We must wait."

The feather of dust vanished for a time but reappeared again, larger than before. He was almost certain now.

Suddenly the Crows showed signs of excitement.

They were aware, too, of the growing dust cloud. The riders grouped again for a furious assault before the rescuers arrived.

The captain called to his people, "Help is coming, folks! A wagon train at last. Our prayers are answered. Steady, now. The Indians will attack again. Give it to them hot and heavy."

Children cried happily and women wept for joy. The men crouched grimly behind the wagons, their rifles ready.

Finding themselves about to be cheated of their prey, the Crows rushed upon the corral with all the fury of their first attack. But now the defenders fought back with new hope and spirit. The Indians swept in recklessly, their sallies costing them two more warriors.

A small boy thrust his head through the torn canvas of his hiding place. "The wagons . . . I can see the wagons coming," he called.

A cheer rang out from the corral, a shout of triumph that carried out to the frenzied Indians.

The Crows saw they were beaten and broke off their attack before the horsemen came within rifle range. With a last defiant yell they rode out of sight behind the mesa, carrying their dead with them.

"Thank God, you got here in time," the captain said as he stepped out of the corral to greet the riders. About him, women wept their thanks, children leaped for joy and smiling men shook hands with their rescuers.

The two parties made camp for the night and at daybreak pushed on to meet together the perils of the trail ahead.

They rarely outdistanced trouble and danger. Although Fort Laramie lay behind, the hardest part of the journey still faced them. They must climb the rising slope to South Pass, beyond which lay the Wasatch Mountains, Fort Hall, the lava beds along the Snake River, more mountains and then the Columbia river valley.

People married, were born and died along the way. The hardships were too great for the very old and the weak. Wooden crosses and wagon wheels marked the graves, like mileposts in a dreary land.

The strong survived to build new homes in the Oregon country. A few, still hunting for something better, drifted down to the Mexican territory of California.

The nation's attention was drawn to the Southwest even while the rush to Oregon was drawing thousands of people away from the East. There was trouble with Mexico along the Rio Grande, trouble that brought on a revolt in Texas and then a war.

Many Americans had settled in Texas when it was still a Mexican state. They tired of foreign rule and fought for freedom. After they gained that, they made

Texas a part of the United States. This action only increased the friction along the border, and in 1846 Mexico and the United States went to war.

The American commander Colonel Stephen W. Kearny moved west from Fort Leavenworth with an army that took New Mexico with little more effort than a social call on the governor at Santa Fe.

Fighting several battles on its march westward from Santa Fe, the United States Army defeated the Mexican forces. By 1848 the United States had added New Mexico, Arizona and California to its expanding West.

To guard the new frontier and to check the growing boldness of the Plains Indians, the Army scattered its posts over hundreds of miles. Suspicion and ill feeling between white and red men increased. Where it would lead, no one could tell.

Something was about to happen in California that would end forever the Indians' hope of keeping their hunting grounds to themselves. A westward stampede, greater even than the rush to Oregon, was about to begin.

CHAPTER 6

The Big Discovery

JOHN AUGUSTUS SUTTER waddled across the courtyard inside his adobe brick fort toward a row of workshops against the opposite wall. Behind him stood his house, flanked by quarters for his workmen.

As he passed the open gate looking out upon the American River a quarter of a mile away, he paused to glimpse a section of his vast wheat fields. An orchard and vineyard lay near by—and stretching far out of sight were his pastures for thousands of cattle, horses, mules, sheep and hogs.

Sutter nodded his balding head in frank satisfaction. All this had become his in less than ten years. Coming to California as a pioneer in 1839, he built up this rich estate on a little-known frontier.

His grant from the Mexican governor included forty-eight thousand acres that spread out from the juncture of the American and Sacramento rivers. With a colony of five white men and ten Indians he built his fort, planted his fields and started his flocks.

Now he gave work to scores of people and ruled over his "empire" like a good-natured king. Trappers, hunters, emigrants and wanderers of all sorts came to

Sutter's trading post, sure of a welcome and glad to buy the produce of his fields and workshops. Sutter's Nueva Helvetia, today the site of California's capital, was something to make any man proud.

"General" Sutter, everyone called him—the thought made him smile to himself. He had led a force from his colony to help the Mexican governor during an Indian uprising. Since then he had been hailed as "general."

Sutter remembered finally what he had set out to do and he shuffled on to the carpenter's shop in a corner of the fort. "Oh, Jim," he called, stepping into the doorway. His short, fat body almost closed the opening. Squinting into the gloomy room he said, "Are you in here, Jim?"

A lean and grizzled man fitting legs to a new table straightened up from his work. "What is it, General?" James Marshall said. He was Sutter's Jack-of-all-trades, able to build a house, prune a tree or shoe a horse.

"Jim, it's time we had our own flour mill to grind our wheat," Sutter said. "We can't keep up with the demand since all these people are drifting down from Oregon. I want you to start work on a new mill."

"We'll need more than adobe bricks for a flour mill," Marshall said. "We must have lumber—and there aren't enough boards around here to build a chicken coop."

Sutter rubbed the gray fringe around his ears.

"Well then, Jim, suppose we put up a sawmill and cut our own lumber. We should have had one long ago."

"There's no timber around the fort," Marshall objected. "We'll have to go back in the hills."

"Take an Indian guide and a couple of other men to scout for a good site. There's good timber up along the American River."

On May 16, 1847, Marshall and his aids left the fort. After riding forty-five miles along the south fork they found a suitable spot for a dam and mill. Beginning work at once, a crew under Marshall finished their work the next January. However, they still needed a tailrace through which to lead the water back to the river after it had turned the power wheel.

Marshall found that he could save time and labor by loosening the earth with a pick and then letting the river current wash it away.

On the afternoon of January 24, 1848, while walking beside the tailrace, Marshall noticed several yellow specks in the gravel. He picked up one of the pieces, found it surprisingly heavy and soft. After biting into it he pounded it with a stone and was able to mash it.

"Is it gold?" Marshall asked himself. It was too surprising to believe—and yet the more he examined the metal, the more convinced he became. At suppertime that evening he said to his fellow workmen, "I'm not sure, boys, but I think I have found a gold mine."

One of the men laughed and said, "We wouldn't have that kind of luck."

All were interested enough, however, to go with Marshall the next morning to look for more flakes. They picked up four ounces of the metal, which the cook boiled. The pieces turned brighter than ever.

Sure now that he had found gold, Marshall pleaded with his men. "Go back to work, boys, and don't say a word about this. I'm going down to the fort and tell the general."

With the metal in his pocket he mounted a horse and raced forty-five miles through a heavy rain to Sutter's fort. Soaking wet and covered with mud, he entered Sutter's office, locked the door and spoke in whispers. His manner alarmed the general.

"What's happened, Marshall?" Sutter said.

For answer, Marshall dumped the contents of a small bag upon Sutter's desk. "Look at that, General. We've found gold!"

Sutter frowned as he fingered the cluster of yellow grains. "I can't believe— But we'll soon find out. We'll test it and see if it's really gold."

First using acid and then weighing it on small drugstore scales, Sutter quickly proved that Marshall was right. It was the precious metal that set men wild, the first gold reported in California.

The next day Sutter rode to the sawmill and joined Marshall in exploring a wider area. They found gold

"We've *found gold!*" *cried Marshall*

almost everywhere they looked along the American River. Both were sure now it was an important discovery. Yet Sutter only shook his head sadly. "This is terrible, Jim. I wish you'd never found the plagued stuff."

"You wish—" Marshall stared at Sutter in unbelief. "You can't mean what you say, General. Why, we've found gold. *Gold!* It will make us rich."

"Oh, it probably won't amount to much. I've heard of these gold strikes before . . . never excited me. We've just started building the flour mill. I want my workmen busy on that, not digging around in the river for gold. The discovery will do us more harm than good. Jim, we must keep it to ourselves."

"The sawmill crew knows about it already." Marshall said. "How are you going to keep them quiet?"

"I'll have a talk with them," Sutter said. He called the crew together and ordered them to stay on their jobs and not to breathe a word about the gold. Unwillingly at first, the men finally promised to say nothing for the next six weeks.

But the secret was too big, too exciting, to be smothered. At the sawmill camp the workmen could not keep their minds on their jobs—and they gathered the little nuggets whenever they had a chance. Sutter tried to keep them isolated but the news spread to the fort. A teamster, his tongue loosened by whisky, told a storekeeper. So it went on, from one to another, until the rumors reached San Francisco.

Unready to believe it at first, its citizens had proof in April when nuggets and gold dust began to appear. Like fire spreading in dry grass the news raced up and down the coast—to Monterey, Los Angeles and San Diego, even flashing northward into Oregon.

As though on signal, everyone dropped his work and rushed to Sutter's sawmill. The stampede was on.

CHAPTER 7

Gold Fever

GENERAL SUTTER'S sawmill workers forgot their pledge. As fast as they could gather enough gold —accepted by traders at eight dollars an ounce—they bought pans, shovels, picks, boots, blankets, flour, beef and bacon and became miners.

His field hands likewise quit their jobs to dig gold and his wheat and fruit stood unharvested. His mills were never finished—even the Indians in his colony had caught the fever. Why work when it was easier to find gold?

The frenzy to reach the gold field practically emptied San Francisco. Storekeepers closed their shops, homes were deserted, churches emptied. Clerks, lawyers, judges, merchants dropped their work and joined the rush. Even the newspaper was silent, for the printers were gone.

Farmers abandoned their land, soldiers deserted their ranks, sailors and officers alike jumped ship and clawed the earth for its yellow lucre.

The miners used simple tools—either a tin pan or a set of sluice boxes—when working beside the river. Into his shallow pan a miner placed a shovelful of gold-

The miners used simple tools

bearing gravel and then scooped it full of water. By rocking the pan back and forth he caused the water to swirl over the edge, washing out all but the heavy metal.

To separate gold from the gravel with sluice boxes, a small group of men usually worked together. They first built three or four wooden troughs and set them end to end on an incline, one overlapping the other. Several crossbars, called riffles, were nailed upon the floor of the boxes.

After a quantity of gravel had been shoveled into the topmost trough, a stream of water was turned into the sluice boxes. As the gravel washed away, the riffles caught the gold.

Sutter's fear that the discovery of gold on his place would harm him became a reality. His property melted away and within a few years he was reduced from the ruler of a great estate to a bankrupt homesteader.

The first arrivals staked claims around Sutter's fort. As the area became crowded, later prospectors explored farther up the American and Sacramento rivers. They found gold almost everywhere. Here was evidence enough that the California strike was a rich one, rich enough to spread the news around the world.

After President James Knox Polk reported to Congress late in 1848 on the extent of the discovery, the gold craze swept the East. Everyone wanted to head west but the problem was how to reach the Pacific quickly enough.

It was now winter and the overland trails were closed. The sea routes remained—around South America and up the long Pacific Coast in sailing vessels, or by way of the Isthmus of Panama. The voyage around Cape Horn took from six to nine months. It required less time to sail to the isthmus, cross the jungles of Panama—on a mule or afoot in about five days—then board another vessel to continue the voyage to California.

Although sea travel was expensive the cost did not stop bankers, professional men, merchants, manufacturers, students, artists, mechanics and even a few women from booking passage on every available ship heading west. Vessels leaving Atlantic coast ports in December, 1848, went around the Horn and reached San Francisco in early July. Before the month was out fifty-four ships were anchored in the harbor. Vessels from ports the world over soon joined them.

Often it was the last voyage of such ships because crews and officers headed for the gold diggings with their passengers. In another year five hundred vessels stood rotting in the bay, deserted by their sailors.

Once at the gold fields the newcomers found the cost of tools and food sky high. A dollar shovel was priced at ten. Pans, picks, knives and crowbars were ten times their former price. Clothing was equally costly and hard to get.

Flour sold for four hundred dollars a barrel, sugar and coffee four dollars a pound. A fifty-dollar rowboat brought five hundred dollars. Only the richness of the gold strike made it possible for the miners to pay such prices.

The spring of 1849 brought a fever of excitement to the frontier of the Missouri River. Westbound travelers, instead of arriving by the usual hundreds, came by the thousands, then the tens of thousands. Oxen, wagons and people jammed the streets of river towns. Each day steamers unloaded eager adventurers driven by the mad hope of getting rich. Their only talk was about gold—California gold. They made up the army known as the Forty-niners.

As soon as the prairie grass was long enough to feed their livestock, the gold hunters began their journey.

Copying the earlier method of travel they moved out in long trains.

A count made at St. Joseph, Missouri, showed that by mid-May over twenty-five hundred wagons had been ferried across the river. Fifteen hundred more waited their turns. Before the approaching winter stopped overland travel one hundred thousand Forty-niners had reached California.

While most of the overland gold hunters were bold young men drawn largely from American farms, the story of California's gold reached across the Atlantic and soon hundreds of Europeans joined the adventure. They met hardships and suffering beyond belief. Not all of the hopeful ones finished the trip.

The travelers knew nothing about the rugged life in the open. They were soft and inexperienced. "Tenderfeet" and "greenhorns," the veterans of the trail called them.

Their troubles began before they were well onto the Kansas prairies. Wagons broke down, livestock became crippled, overloaded and poorly made vehicles had to be lightened. There was no fear of losing the trail because it soon became littered with useless and unneeded articles thrown aside at every stop.

Breakdowns failed to discourage many. If wagons could not be repaired, the owners broke up the wheels to make pack saddles of the spokes and piled what gear they could manage upon the backs of mules or oxen. One party reported it passed the wreckage of eleven such wagons in half a day. In one twenty-four-mile stretch, seventeen abandoned wagons and twenty-seven dead oxen were counted. The carcasses of eight lay in one heap at the roadside.

The Indians were far from idle during this invasion of their hunting grounds. They accepted the challenge in the way they met all enemies—by killing, scalping, looting and burning. In this kind of warfare they had no equals. Their surprise raids sometimes wiped out whole companies of men. Wreckage of wagons and bodies of their victims were left behind as a warning to others.

Cholera, a dread disease that spread from party to party along the trail, broke out when the first trains left the Missouri River. After suffering severe pain the victims rarely lived longer than a few days. Five thousand graves lined the road between the Missouri and the hills beyond Fort Laramie.

Greater physical hardships faced the gold rushers on the second half of their journey. Once past Fort Hall in Idaho or Salt Lake in Utah, they had to cross Humboldt Valley in Nevada—where heat, dust and lack of water and food caused many deaths daily.

Stock died as grass and water vanished. Oxen dropped under their yokes and thousands of Forty-niners either had to turn back to Salt Lake or force themselves on afoot, taking chances on dying from thirst and starvation. Those able to finish the three-thousand-mile journey arrived at their goal tough and rugged men, fit to endure the hardships of mining camp life.

In their frantic search for new and bigger pockets of gold, the miners pushed ever farther into the California wilderness. Every gulch and mountain stream was explored. For shelter, the prospectors dug holes in riverbanks or threw together a few logs, tree boughs and bits of canvas. That done they set to work at once, panning the gravel or building sluice boxes for placer mining.

Wherever a few hundred miners settled down, the storekeeper, the laundryman, the lunchroom operator, the gambler and whisky seller came along, eager to relieve the digger of his gold.

Crude towns grew up around the richest gold strikes. Tents and shacks were built in zigzag rows at the bottom of a ravine or gulch. Planks resting on barrels or tree stumps served as shelves and counters for the businessmen.

A foot or wagon trail weaved between the blocks of crude buildings. The street oozed mud when wet and sent up choking clouds of dust when dry. Such camps sprang up almost overnight on the Mokelumne River, at Auburn, at Downieville, at Columbia, at Ophir, Yuba, Dogtown, in French Ravine, in dozens of other spots. Wherever gold was found in promising color a camp took root, only to be abandoned when word of a newer and richer strike elsewhere flashed through the settlement.

The miners rarely were without company of an evil sort. Almost before a camp had a name, the worst types of men and women flocked to it, interested only in separating the miner from his gold.

Criminals from the petty thief to the worst murderer flocked to the diggings. In the first wild rush to Sutter's mill, the jails were emptied along with business places and offices.

Crime and lawlessness were soon out of hand. There was no police force or courts to deal with the outlaws. Yet there were enough honest and honorable men digging gold ready to strike back at the criminals.

Banding together in groups that became known as vigilance committees, they hunted down the robbers and killers. Setting up their own courts, they held swift trials and punished the guilty before the sun set. Hanging was the usual penalty. Gradually order took hold in the mining camps as the villains fled the vigilantes' wrath—if lucky enough to escape the noose.

Not all acts done in the name of the vigilantes were in the interest of law and order, however. Innocent men were sometimes punished by overeager miners ready to vent their anger on the handiest victim. In other instances, deceitful men worked under the cloak of the vigilantes to drive away—or even murder—men who blocked their criminal plans.

In the eight years after gold was discovered at Sutter's sawmill, not less than four hundred and fifty million dollars' worth was dug from California's soil. Some miners became rich, more threw away their wealth to gamblers and by wasteful living. Hundreds endured the hard life only long enough to earn a farm, pay off a mortgage or save a stake to start a business. Many Forty-niners returned to the East as poor as they left. Yet the thousands who remained in California made up a vigorous group—and their plea for statehood was soon granted.

The stampede to California drew the nation's attention upon the West. The Great Plains and the Rockies were no longer unknown to multitudes of easterners. By 1850 the United States had pushed its frontier to the Pacific Coast in one great leap. But there was still a vast area between the Missouri River and California—ruled largely by hostile Indians—that was yet to be conquered.

CHAPTER 8

Peace or War?

LIKE sailboats bobbing on a rough sea, the covered wagons streamed out over the western trails in endless files. Settlements appeared on land the Indians had always ruled. Trading posts and army forts dotted riverbanks deep inside the red men's territory. Wherever white men advanced, the Indians' game retreated.

The white men's promises made to the tribes years before were broken. The chiefs told their warriors, "The palefaces talk with a crooked tongue. We must drive them out of our hunting grounds. Our villages will die if we do not make war to stop them."

The braves fought fiercely to turn back the white tide. But the invaders came in ever-growing numbers; raids and attacks increased week by week. Bitterness seethed on both sides.

To put a stop to the warfare Thomas Fitzpatrick, the Indian agent at Fort Laramie on the upper Platte River, called the tribes to a council to make peace. Sullen and distrustful, the Indians were in no hurry to smoke the peace pipe.

Under Fitzpatrick's urging they began at last to

appear at the fort. The Sioux and Assiniboins, the Arikaras, the Gros Ventres and the Crows came from the north, the Shoshoni bands from the west.

They came by the hundreds, then by the thousands. They would show the whites how strong they were. The Fort Laramie Council of 1851 became the greatest gathering of Plains Indians ever known.

The mighty chiefs, Crazy Horse, Red Cloud and Man-Afraid-of-His-Horse, led their people to the council. They were dressed in war bonnets of white eagle feathers, leggings of doeskin with beadwork or of white elkskin glistening with quills. Painted fearsomely they rode like emperors on the finest horses of their herds. Soured by the wrongs they had suffered they came in an ugly mood.

Tepees covered the river bottom and the grassy slopes around the fort. Warriors, squaws, boys, girls and papooses moved about ceaselessly. Dogs raced through the villages, barking and snarling. Vast pony herds grazed beyond the noisy camps.

At the council house inside the fort the great men of the tribes met with the white chiefs. Gravely the leaders listened to the message from the Great White Father.

"Our people seek new homes beyond the mountains," the white men said. "Their path lies through the Sioux country. You must allow us to build forts and roads. We must protect our people against the

Tepees covered the grassy slopes around the fort

tribes who will not make peace. You will be paid for the land you give up."

Wrapped in a blood-red blanket, Chief Red Cloud arose to answer. A huge man, he addressed the council with dignity and firmness.

"The trail to Oregon has caused much trouble," Red Cloud said. "Now, instead of closing that trail, the Great White Father wishes to make others. The roads our white brothers build drive away the buffalo and other game. They bring hunger to the red men. Our squaws and our children will starve. Yet we wish peace with our white brothers. We believe they will keep their word and not make war on us. We will let you build your roads and forts."

Crazy Horse, slender and handsome, dark as polished walnut, arose to voice his mistrust. Other chiefs orated at length and finally, after many days of talk, a treaty was signed.

In this treaty the Sioux agreed that their range lay north of the Platte River. The Cheyennes and Arapahoes accepted the region between the Platte and Arkansas rivers for their hunting grounds.

The tribes also recognized the government's right to build roads and posts where it wished. And attacks on wagon trains would stop, they said.

In return, Fitzpatrick and the other United States agents promised that the tribes would be paid half a million dollars a year for fifty years. Out of this sum,

"We wish peace with our white brothers," said Chief Red Cloud

settlers who had suffered from Indian attacks were to be paid damages.

The treaty went to the United States Senate for approval. That body changed the number of yearly payments from fifty to fifteen. Actually, the tribes received even fewer than that in the troubled years ahead.

Yet the treaty had its desired effect, even though briefly. The Indians kept the peace, except for minor flare-ups, until events took it out of their hands.

During the peaceful years freight wagon operations grew into the chief business on the plains. The number of traders hauling goods to Santa Fe increased yearly. Other wagon outfits freighted supplies to army forts and outposts.

One of the most successful wagon masters was Alexander Majors, who started as a Santa Fe trader. On his first venture into the Southwest he made the round trip in ninety-two days, the fastest on record.

Majors ran his trains under rules strange to the trail. He required each teamster to sign a pledge not to beat or abuse the oxen and not to drink, curse, gamble or quarrel with others of the crew. More surprising to old-time freighters—Majors' train rested on Sundays. His wagons came back in good repair and his animals fat and strong.

The rapid growth of Majors' outfit caught the notice of William H. Russell and William B. Waddell, who were also engaged in freighting. They asked Majors' help in forming a company large enough to haul all the Army's supplies.

The result was the firm of Russell, Majors and Waddell, who became the freight masters of the plains. In their best years they employed four thousand men, forty thousand oxen, thirty-five hundred wagons and hundreds of horses and mules. Their warehouses, corrals, blacksmith shops, wagon parks and supply stores took on the size of small cities. Their trains traveled the West from Santa Fe to Utah, while profits reached three hundred thousand dollars a year.

It was time now to heed California's appeal for a

faster mail service. Letters and papers took months to reach the Pacific Coast by the sea and Panama Canal route. A stagecoach line to carry passengers and mail from Missouri to California was urged to fill the gap.

John Butterfield, a pioneer in the express business, undertook to run stagecoaches every two weeks from St. Louis to San Francisco by way of El Paso and Los Angeles. Each trip would take twenty-five days. The new line was called the Overland Mail Company.

This southern route was favored over the Central Trail through Salt Lake City, even though it was much longer, because it would not be closed in winter by mountain snows.

To carry mail, express and passengers over this roadless expanse, Butterfield bought a fleet of coaches—tough, speedy carriages that could withstand even a tumble down a canyon slope without smashing up.

The driver rode on a seat high above the three teams of mules that raced along at a gallop. Under his feet was a boxlike space, called a boot, in which parcels were carried. A larger boot for mail, express and baggage was attached to the rear of the body.

Inside the coach were three seats holding three passengers each. When more had to be hauled they were jammed inside or forced to share the driver's seat. As many as fourteen passengers, besides the driver, were sometimes crowded aboard.

Mail took first place, however, and when the shipment was unusually heavy the passengers had to make the best of it. The overflow went inside the coach, under the seats and upon the floor. During such times the riders sprawled over the bags, a position that added no comfort to the jolting and swaying journey. Surplus mail was sometimes roped between the axles and slung under the body, where it was likely to become soaked at the first river crossing.

Before the stage line could begin operating, Butterfield sent out crews to set up relay stations ten miles apart. At such places a corral was built for spare mules and a crude cabin for the stock tender, who supplied fresh animals as the coaches reached the station.

Several relay points along the route were known as home stations, places where passengers could buy quick meals and where blacksmiths made repairs on coaches. There were no long stops, either day or night, and the mules had to average nearly five miles an hour to cover the hundred-mile stretch marked out for each day's run. At the end of the hard trip the passengers were in greater need of attention than the mules.

On September 15, 1858, the first stages took to the road, one from each end of the line. The California coach reached St. Louis a few hours under the twenty-five-day limit. When wired the news in Washington, President James Buchanan replied to Butterfield, "I cordially congratulate you upon the result. It is a glorious triumph for civilization and the Union."

CHAPTER 9

"Pikes Peak or Bust"

A BEARDED miner rode into Omaha, Nebraska, one cold January day in 1859 carrying six quills, or rolls of bark, filled with gold dust and small nuggets. Proudly, he held up the yellow metal for an excited crowd to see.

"Where did you get the gold, pardner?" a man called out.

"Dug it out of a sandbank at the mouth of Cherry Creek, out Pikes Peak way," the miner said. "Found it last fall, just before the freeze-up. Boys, there's lots more out there, believe me."

"Then it's true," another man said. "For months we've been hearing reports of a new discovery out there."

"Of course it's true," the miner said. "I'm going back there come spring and make myself rich."

"I missed out on the California stampede," a listener said. "But not this time. I'm heading for Pikes Peak just as soon as the trails open."

"Same here. . . ." "Me, too," other men cried.

The news flashed across the nation. Newspapers carried accounts of the discovery and printed direc-

Gold discovery out Pikes Peak way!

tions for reaching the area. That was more than enough to set off another stampede of easterners hoping to get rich quick.

Conditions were right for another westward rush. The country was in the grip of hard times. A panic had forced banks to close, factories to shut down and crops to rot in the fields for lack of markets. Thousands of people were out of jobs. Why sit idly at home when there was free gold to be picked up in the shadow of the Rockies?

Besides, the new gold field was easy to reach. It lay only seven hundred miles from the Missouri, free of desert and mountain travel. Wagon trains had been using the Platte Trail for years; a stagecoach line to Colorado was about to start. The cost was far less than the Forty-niners paid to reach California.

Crowds began to gather along the Missouri River. Their camps lined the stream from Independence to Council Bluffs. Steamboats, sometimes two and three a day, arrived at Fort Leavenworth, Kansas, to pour hundreds of people into the streets. Storekeepers, wheelwrights, blacksmiths and stockmen were overrun by crowds looking for food and outfits to make the overland trip.

The stampede became more frantic than the rush to California. Those in the biggest hurry scrambled for seats in stagecoaches making their first journeys over the Platte Trail. Travelers unable to find prairie schooners bought light carriages or used pack mules to move their gear. Scores went by horseback and a few set out pushing wheelbarrows or pulling hand carts.

By April, twenty-five thousand gold hunters had left the river border for Colorado. Three times as many more followed before the rush ended. For all of them it was "Pikes Peak or Bust."

So sure were some people that a new district of the West was about to be settled that they moved goods to open stores, printing presses for newspapers and machinery for sawmills. Everyone felt certain of becoming rich.

The hardships suffered by the Forty-niners were faced again in this stampede. Few had knowledge of travel across the plains. Their wagons broke down and they became sick and hungry. The Indians, dismayed by this new mass of white men, attacked the trains, killing and plundering in their fury.

The first easterners to reach Cherry Creek found that miners who had wintered in the West had already formed a town and named it Denver City. It became the supply center of the region and the end of the stage line.

The newcomers who worked the creeks of eastern Colorado uncovered gold in very small amounts. The loose grains and dust were soon panned out. The rich deposits, it was learned months later, were back in the mountains, deep in quartz lodes where stamp mills were needed to crush the rock.

Such mining called not only for experience but capital with which to buy machinery and chemicals. The green miners had neither—and their hopes for wealth died in a few weeks.

The boom broke before the last of the west-bound miners reached the Denver area. Disappointed crowds on their way home met hopeful hundreds still toiling westward across the plains. Before 1859 ended, more than half of the Pikes Peak miners were "busted" and were straggling back east.

As did the stampede to California, the rush to Colorado speeded the opening of the West. Many hardy and daring men saw the plains and mountains for the first time. Unable to find gold around Denver, they set out as prospectors to explore the Rockies. Moving into unknown valleys and across the plateaus, they found land, streams and timber that tempted them as much as did the gold. They settled down—and the West became their home.

The Pikes Peak rush also helped to bring the stagecoach into more general use upon the plains. The line to Denver was started by William Russell against the advice of his freight business partners, Alexander Majors and William Waddell. They feared the line would never pay but Russell expected to profit from the gold mine trade.

With John S. Jones, a new partner, Russell borrowed large sums to buy eight hundred mules and fifty Concord coaches—and then set up a string of relay stations. They called their line the Leavenworth and Pikes Peak Express Company.

The carriages were the most rugged yet—and the finest to be had, each costing twenty-four hundred dollars. Their wheels were bright yellow and the bodies red or green, with fancy figures and designs gilded upon the woodwork. Landscapes and other colorful scenes were painted on the doors. Nothing more elegant or gaudy ever appeared on the Great Plains.

The Pikes Peak line charged twenty-five cents to carry letters and ten cents for newspapers, besides the regular United States postage rate of three cents per half ounce on first-class mail. But there were rarely enough passengers to keep the coaches filled.

The appearance of the "painted wagons" awed the Indians at first, but they soon found it great sport to attack the speeding carriages. More than one coach ended a run with its handsome paintings studded with arrows or splintered by rifle bullets.

It was during this period that Julesburg became the most famous "home station" of the stage line. Drawing to it the toughest characters on the plains, it grew into a rowdy, unruly camp where few days passed without some gunman sending a victim to Boot Hill.

Bandits harassed stages and freight wagons to such an extent that the notorious Joseph "Jack" Slade was hired to clean out the riffraff. One day he clashed with "Old Jules" Reni, who emptied two barrels of bird shot into Slade. That "peace officer" immediately shot Jules to death, cut off his ears and nailed them up to dry. He later wore one for a watch charm.

The Leavenworth and Pikes Peak Express Company lost money from the start—and Russell and Jones could not meet their notes. To save what they could of the stage line, Russell's freighting partners paid the bills and the company became a part of the freight firm's empire.

Without a mail contract, Russell, Majors and Waddell knew that a stage line was a poor risk. In order to compete with Butterfield's Overland Mail Company, they took over a wobbly line carrying mail between Denver and Salt Lake City and formed the Central Overland California and Pikes Peak Express.

Now their stages ran from Fort Leavenworth to Utah. But business was bad. They sank deeper into debt and soon the line's popular name became "Clean Out of Cash and Poor Pay." The venture helped to speed their ruin.

Meantime, the citizens of California were clambering for still faster mail service. Butterfield's stages on the long southern route took twenty-five days one way. Why not bring the mail over the shorter central route through Fort Laramie, Salt Lake City and Sacramento—the gold trail to California?

Here was the chance the three partners had missed when Butterfield won the United States mail contract in 1857. They would prove that the mountain passes could be kept open in winter. Not with stagecoaches—they had a more daring plan.

By mounting riders on fast horses to race in relays—day and night, over mountains, desert and plains—the mail would be carried nearly two thousand miles from the Missouri River to San Francisco in ten days. This was to be a pony express.

Impossible, a good many persons said. Californians had the same doubt but they gave the plan full support. Here was promise of news, letters and express from the East two weeks faster than by stage. The entire nation waited with keen interest for the pony express to begin.

CHAPTER 10

Ponies Carry the Mail

THE job of getting the pony express started fell to Alexander Majors and picked foremen of the Russell, Majors and Waddell Freight Company. Majors sent these men through the West to buy fast ponies, hire carriers and build relay stations.

When all was ready the pay roll listed eighty riders and four hundred station keepers and helpers to care for four hundred and twenty horses. One hundred and ninety relay points, ten to twelve miles apart, stretched across the West. One hundred thousand dollars had been spent to set up the pony express.

Riders were picked as much for their small size as for their bravery and trust. A few were little more than boys, the others in their late teens and early twenties, while most of them scaled less than one hundred twenty-five pounds. They were paid from one hundred and twenty-five to one hundred and fifty dollars a month.

Special lightweight saddles and mail pouches were used. These saddlebags were called *mochilas*, and consisted of a square of leather that fitted over the horn and cantle. The rider sat upon it, thus holding it in place upon the saddle.

He carried the mail in four locked pouches called *cantinas*, one in each corner of the *mochila*. At each relay point, the *mochila* was pulled off and slipped upon the saddle of the horse waiting to carry the rider to the next station.

Riders were armed only with revolvers and perhaps a bowie knife. They wore slouch hats, buckskin shirts and trousers tucked inside high boots. Bridle, saddle and mailbags weighed thirteen pounds, the mail itself another fifteen or twenty.

Their horses were the best to be had. Because of their speed they outran the fastest Indian ponies, and the rider depended upon his mount to prevent his capture. The company had a rule against fighting unless a man was cornered.

The pony express started on April 3, 1860. St. Joseph, Missouri, was picked for the eastern end because the railroad had reached that city. A great crowd gathered to see the first rider dash away with forty-nine letters, five telegrams and a bundle of newspapers.

At San Francisco a like throng cheered the starting rider. He sped down Market Street to the harbor where the mail was put aboard a river boat and carried to Sacramento. There a waiting horseman took the pouches and began the eastward race.

Riding in relays, each mail carrier covered about

seventy-five miles in seven to eight hours. In that period he changed horses six times, spending less than a minute at each stop. At the end of the division a new rider took over the *mochila*. When a carrier finished his run he had a day's rest, then galloped back to his home station with a fresh pack of mail.

As promised, letters and papers were delivered across the plains and mountains in ten days. California celebrated the event wildly. At Sacramento, stores were closed and all business stopped as the whole town turned out to greet the rider. The mail reached San Francisco in the middle of the night, but the city was wide awake and continued its rejoicing until morning.

Because pony mail rates were five dollars for each half ounce, letters were usually written on tissue paper. However, some bulky business letters carried twenty-five one-dollar pony express stickers and as many United States mail stamps, making the total cost twenty-seven and a half dollars.

The express' receipts for one day often totaled one thousand dollars but expenses were even greater. The company lost money from the start. Russell, Majors and Waddell's only hope of making a profit was through a government mail contract. This they never received.

Indians and highway robbers were always a menace to the riders. Only one was ever captured by the tribes-

Indians were always a menace to the riders of the Pony Express

men, however. Although he was shot and killed, his horse escaped and ran riderless to the next station with the mail.

One of the express riders who later became famous as a scout, hunter and plainsman was William F. Cody, known the world over as Buffalo Bill. When only fourteen years old he carried mail from Red Buttes to Three Crossings, Wyoming, once covering three hundred and twenty-two miles without rest.

An Indian war almost caused the pony express to be abandoned before it was two months old. In their raids the Pah-Ute Indians of Nevada burned relay stations and drove off many valuable horses. Troops had to clear the route of tribesmen and the stations had to be rebuilt before the express could run again. The loss to the express operators totaled seventy-five thousand dollars.

Indians and outlaws, storms, flooded rivers and snow in the mountain passes failed to stop the express after the Pah-Ute War. When drifts became deep, strings of mules were driven out to break the trail and trample the snow into a hard path for the carriers.

Month after month they held to their fast schedule, covering the two thousand miles in ten days during the summer, making it in twelve during the winter. Their best record was set in March, 1861, when they carried President Lincoln's Inaugural Address from St. Joseph, Missouri, to Sacramento, California, in seven days and seventeen hours.

Useful as the express proved itself to be, its life was short because a better means of communication was at hand. The Pacific telegraph, being built eastward from California and westward from Missouri, was about to be linked up.

The telegraph was finished on October 24, 1861, and the last pony rider stepped from his saddle. Now messages could be flashed across the nation in seconds. The costly pony express was out of date, its value at an end.

In its year and a half of operation the fast mail service had closed a wide gap across the nation's frontiers. By linking California more closely to the East during the critical months before the Civil War, it had helped to keep that state in the Union. The express had also proved that an overland road could be kept open the year round. All doubt that a transcontinental railroad would someday be built was at an end.

CHAPTER 11

The Gold Camps Roar

DURING the decade following the California stampede, the amateur gold hunters of 1849 pushed eastward from the Pacific. Now skilled in tracking down veins and pockets of the precious metal, these men scattered through the ranges from Mexico to Canada.

Discoveries were first made between the Rio Grande and Colorado rivers and a mining camp grew up at Tucson. But the southwestern diggings were hard to reach and the constant danger of attack by Apache Indians discouraged a large number of miners from flocking into the area.

One type of camp follower let nothing turn him back. The riffraff driven from California by the vigilantes overran Tucson and made it a hard and vicious settlement. They were joined by troopers from an army column marching from California to New Mexico. The lure of gold had a greater appeal to the deserters than life as a soldier.

Meantime, small discoveries along the old California Trail between Salt Lake and Sacramento had drawn a floating population that founded Carson City in 1858. The next spring a rich strike of silver near Gold Hill, in the Sierra Nevadas just east of Lake Tahoe—followed by the uncovering of the famous Comstock lode—started a new boom that left the Tucson diggings all but forgotten.

The Nevada strike—at California's back door—set off another stampede. Miners crowded into every stagecoach available in their scramble to reach the field. Hundreds too eager to wait their turn left on foot, depending on trading posts along the trail for supplies.

Even while the Nevada excitement was at its peak, news that never failed to stir men's blood came out of the northern Rockies. In the summer of 1860 prospectors had found rich gold deposits along the Clearwater River in Idaho. This was in Indian country, on the reserve of the peaceful and friendly Nez Percé tribes. By treaty with the United States they were to have this land free of any white invasion or settlement. No one but government agents was ever to enter it.

But treaties with red men never stopped the white men when such a pact stood in the way of something they wanted. Now it was gold on the Nez Percés' reserve—and the white men would have it. Despite the Indians' protests, five thousand miners flocked to the fork of the Clearwater and Snake rivers and founded Lewiston in 1861.

Any hope the Indians held that the white men

would quickly scoop up the yellow metal and leave vanished when more deposits were found farther south, on the Salmon River. Mines were next opened at Boise, followed by other strikes. The rush of gold hunters pushed the Nez Percés into the corners of their reservations.

Restless prospectors, always searching for new lodes, began to pry into the mountains of Montana territory. One such party, grumbling over its lack of luck, passed through Alder Gulch while returning to Bannock City. Here they stumbled upon a rich placer.

Sending two men on to Bannock for supplies, the others staked out claims on the floor of the gulch. News of the discovery set off the usual rush. Hundreds of men loaded pack animals with food, shovels and pans and raced to the diggings.

In a few days their crude shelters were scattered for twelve miles—from the mouth of the gulch to Bald Mountain.

As many as could find room settled around the placer, while almost overnight their camp became a bustling community called Virginia City. Within a year it had ten thousand citizens and the usual assortment of stores and places of entertainment.

Like other mining towns, Montana's Virginia City was hammered together without thought of the future. Canvas-walled shops, standing between one-story frame buildings, faced each other across a dirt street rutted by the huge wheels of freight wagons. In front of general stores, dance halls and saloons stood rows of saddle horses.

The lust for gold never failed to breed crime—and Virginia City set a high mark for lawlessness. Gun fights, holdups and murders became so common that law-abiding men were forced to band together for their own safety, just as they did in the California gold field.

Working in secret, these Montana vigilantes struck hard at the gunmen around Bannock and Virginia City. In six weeks they hung twenty-four outlaws and drove dozens more out of the region.

Their action followed a pattern of western life repeated many times—criminals in control until honest men, aroused to fighting anger, brought peace and order to their communities.

For years easterners had been heeding the advice of Horace Greeley, a New York editor, to "Go west, young man, go west." The daring, the impulsive, the seekers after gold and adventure had acted upon that counsel.

Another type of pioneer, more sober and less rash, was also moving out upon the prairies. These were home-seekers, farm families leaving behind hard times and poor soil to hunt for free land on which to build new homes among new neighbors.

Their number was swelled by thousands of Euro-

Almost before the roof was on the cabin, the mother brought out her spinning wheel

peans fleeing from abuse, hunger and a hopeless future. America was the land of opportunity. Great crowds of Scandinavians, Germans, Slavs, Poles and Finns started west as soon as their ships reached American ports. They became the real builders of a strong foundation on which the West could grow.

With their household goods, some chickens, ducks and pigs loaded into a wagon—and a cow or two trailing behind—these settlers pushed into Kansas, Nebraska, Iowa and Minnesota. Miles of rich and level land awaited them in a region claimed only by the Indians.

Upon finding a spot that appealed to them, a family set to work building a shelter, sometimes merely a sod hut or a dugout in a creek bank. If timber was close at hand, logs were cut and a cabin raised.

Almost before the roof was on, the mother brought out her spinning wheel to make yarn of cotton and flax. Clothing and food were products of the homesteaders' own efforts. Game and wild ducks, geese, turkeys, prairie chickens and pigeons were plentiful. An hour's hunt provided a family with meat.

Settlers often took land close together for mutual help and friendship. Few had any money, all wore homemade clothes—and they shared each other's joys and sorrows. They were equals, dealing fairly and honestly with one another.

Hardly a home was without its children. As soon as they were old enough to weed a garden or feed the chickens, they had jobs to do. The girls were taught to spin, cook and sew; the boys plowed, cut hay, tended the cows and helped harvest grain. Children were expected to give almost as much as a grownup to the family's welfare.

There were no schools and few books at first. The pioneer mothers were the teachers and the boys and girls learned to read and write in their own homes.

Young people married early. There were no jobs for girls other than that of housewife. When a young man was ready to have his own farm he married the daughter of one of his neighbors. The marriage was celebrated by the whole neighborhood. All joined in building and furnishing a new home for the young couple.

Enemies of various sorts plagued the homesteaders.

The children had jobs to do

There were years of drought when the hot sun burned up the crops. Grasshoppers and locusts swept across the land to devour every living plant. Prairie fires whipped through dry grass to consume cabins, barns and haystacks.

But the most feared enemies were the Indians. The tribesmen looked upon the settlers as rivals for their hunting grounds. These homesteaders did not make roads over which to reach the Pacific. Once they built their homes and plowed their fields, the Indians were forced farther and farther west.

There were raids in the night upon lonely farm homes. Families were slain, their buildings burned and their livestock stolen. Quarrels between white men and Indians created tension on the frontier that led to a serious outbreak in Iowa.

A dispute between a Sioux and a white farmer over a dog set off the spark that inflamed the Indians' anger. A war party attacked the settlement of Spirit Lake, killed forty-seven whites and took others captive.

Troops sent down from Fort Ridgely, Minnesota, rescued some of the prisoners but it was a feeble show of force. The outraged settlers never felt that the Indians were punished properly.

The Iowa massacre was only a hint of the terror that would soon grip the Minnesota river valley to the north.

CHAPTER 12

Frontier Massacre

FEAR rode high among the white settlers in the Minnesota river valley. For a long time they had worried over the growing unfriendliness of the Sioux under their fiery chief, Little Crow. Their worry turned to alarm when civil war broke out between the North and South.

One question haunted every family. Would the Sioux wait until frontier troops had been called to fight against the South and then fall upon the settlers along the river?

There had been talk of this happening. It was plain that the tribesmen were bitter over many things—loss of their land, the sharp practices of the white traders, impatience over delay in payment of treaty money.

Ten years before, Little Crow, the Sioux's leading chief, had signed the treaty by which the Sioux gave up their territory east of the Red River of the North, Minnesota's western boundary. The Indians, however, had reserved for themselves a strip twenty miles wide along the upper Minnesota river.

In the following years many Sioux took up the white man's ways and tilled the soil, becoming peaceful "farmer" Indians. Most of them, nevertheless, clung to their tepees and blankets, living off the land. The "blanket" Indians never softened in their hatred for the white settlers who now crowded upon them by the thousands. They mocked their brothers who gave up their native customs.

The Indians' ill feeling was especially keen against the white traders with whom they dealt. The tribesmen, buying blankets, flour, pork, ammunition and other needs on credit, were always in debt. They were cheated by high prices and short weight. The first four hundred thousand dollars received for their land went to the traders to satisfy claims against the tribesmen.

The action of the settlers themselves further angered the Indians. White farmers had moved upon Sioux holdings before the treaty had been approved by the United States Senate and payment made for the land.

Although Little Crow had discarded his native dress for white man's clothes and had joined a church, he never softened toward the invaders who had wronged his people.

Because they had no money the tribesmen were going hungry. They had waited since spring for a keg of gold due them as a treaty payment. Its failure to arrive was one more grievance laid at the white man's door.

About this time troops stationed at Fort Ridgely

The Indians' ill feeling was especially keen against the white traders

had marched to Fort Snelling, one hundred miles down river, on their way to the Civil War. Only a company of Minnesota infantry was left to man Fort Ridgely. The valley residents were troubled, because that fort was their last outpost of protection. What would happen now?

Almost by accident the Indians' smoldering temper was fanned into flame. It happened on Sunday, August 17, 1862, when four Sioux braves found a nestful of eggs on a farm in Meeker County, far north of the Minnesota River.

Warned by a companion not to touch the white man's property, one of the braves dashed the eggs to the ground and accused the other of being a coward.

Dared to show his bravery, the Sioux led his companions in an attack upon the farm family. In a few minutes they killed five persons. Next they stole their victims' horses and rode to Chief Shakopee's village to boast of their deeds. This camp was six miles from the Lower Sioux agency, a settlement of white traders and the residence of a man who handled the government's business with the tribes.

News of the killings created excitement among Shakopee's people. Fearful that trouble would result, the chief took the four guilty braves before Little Crow, the Sioux's head chief. They found Little Crow abed at his home near the agency.

He listened gravely to Chief Shakopee's report of

the killings. Turning to the culprits he said, "You have made war on the whites. They will seek revenge and there will be blood shed. The Great White Father in Washington will stop payments on our lands."

Looking at Shakopee he ordered, "Call a council of the chiefs and warriors. We must decide what we are to do."

Messengers hurriedly called the tribal leaders to the council. Through the night they argued hotly. A few of the chiefs—especially Big Eagle, Wabasha and Wacouta—pleaded that the Sioux make peace with the whites before it was too late. But not many would listen.

"We have suffered many wrongs from the whites," angry leaders argued. "They are trying to push us out of the whole valley. Most of the paleface soldiers have left Fort Ridgely. Now is the time to strike."

"Kill the white men!" the warriors demanded.

Chief Little Crow debated his own course. He knew that his people would be punished for the murders that had just taken place. When the whites hit back they would see little difference between "farmer" and "blanket" Indians. Both would suffer in a war of revenge.

The time had come for the Sioux to protect their property and rights. If they waited longer it would be too late. Little Crow joined the group urging the long-delayed attack upon the settlers.

The council voted to go to war.

At once the warriors made themselves ready. Smearing themselves with war paint they rode down upon the near-by Lower Sioux agency, striking first at the hated white traders.

The raids then spread to the farms around the Lower Sioux agency. When word of the outbreak reached Fort Ridgely, fifteen miles to the east, about twenty-five infantrymen set out for the agency. They were ambushed and shot down like sheep. A few stragglers returned to the fort. The fort commander sent a horseman to Fort Snelling, a hundred miles to the east, with an appeal for help.

When the alarm spread to more distant areas, families fled from their homes to shelter in villages and in Fort Ridgely.

Once he had given consent to the uprising, Chief Little Crow led his warriors in the most daring raids. The first fighting had crippled the valley's only force of soldiers, the handful of men at Fort Ridgely. Little Crow looked toward New Ulm as a tempting prize.

The German village of twelve hundred residents lay twenty miles below the fort. Situated on a prairie back from the river, it lay open to attack.

At midafternoon the villagers were surprised to see a large war party sweeping upon it. The cry, "Indians! The Sioux are coming!" spread panic among the citizens. Women and children fled into their homes. Men grabbed rifles and ran to meet the attackers.

The first rush almost overwhelmed the little force. Firing from behind barns and sheds at the edge of the village, they finally checked the warriors. Arrows and lead ripped through doors and windows; several defenders fell dead, a dozen were wounded.

Terror ruled New Ulm for an hour and a half. Just as Little Crow and his braves gathered for another assault, a heavy rainstorm swept over the village. The Indians vanished as quickly as they had appeared.

The men gathered to discuss their danger. "Little Crow will come back," they agreed. "He'll round up more of his rascals for the next attack. We must have help."

It was decided a messenger would have to ride to Traverse de Sioux, fifteen miles to the east, for volunteers to aid New Ulm. It would be a dangerous mission, through an area full of Indians on the warpath. Who would go?

Seventeen-year-old Rudolph Schultz volunteered. On a borrowed horse he set out in the dusk.

Instead of renewing his attack on New Ulm at once, Little Crow decided upon a bolder move. He had a force of thirteen hundred warriors under him now. With this band he believed he could take Fort Ridgely. Once the fort was destroyed, nothing could stop the Sioux's sweep of the valley. They could overrun Mankato, St. Peter and the other settlements along the river—right down to St. Paul itself.

The attack began the day after the raid upon New Ulm. Yelling savagely, the warriors rode confidently against the stockade. A thunder of rifle fire and the boom of a cannon greeted Little Crow and his braves. Surprised by the strong defense the Sioux broke and turned back.

Little Crow expected an easy victory here. Instead, he found the fort full of volunteers and settlers who had fled to it for protection. Their rifles kept the warriors at a distance. After several futile assaults the braves began sniping attacks that continued throughout the day.

At daylight the next morning Little Crow rallied his warriors for a fresh charge upon the fort. But in the night many braves had slipped away to plunder abandoned homes and to raid farms still untouched. This was a kind of warfare dearer to the savage heart.

The Fort Ridgely defenders held off Little Crow for another day. Realizing that he could not take it by storm, the chief turned back to an easier prize—New Ulm.

Uniting his force with that led by another chief, Big Eagle, Little Crow renewed his attack upon the German settlement. Again the Sioux hit boldly. With flaming arrows they set two hundred buildings afire. Despite repeated charges, however, they could not overrun the village. The defenders' fire was stronger than in the Sioux's first assault.

Rudolph Schultz's ride for help had brought Judge Charles E. Flandrau and a party of citizen-soldiers to New Ulm's aid. The battle dragged on for two days at a cost of twenty-nine settlers dead and many wounded. Little Crow's braves suffered heavily, too, and at last they gave up the fight.

After the Sioux vanished, Judge Flandrau called the defenders together. "We must get the women and children away before the Indians return with a larger force," he said. "Round up every wagon you can. Tonight we will abandon New Ulm and head for Mankato."

Working swiftly, the men had the wagons ready by dark. When the wounded and the womenfolk were aboard, the long column rolled away toward Mankato, twenty-five miles down the river.

"Where are the troops?" the settlers still far from help asked each other anxiously. "Why have no soldiers been sent from Fort Snelling to save us?"

While the whites waited for help the Sioux moved farther up the river valley. Thousands were now on the warpath—killing and burning mercilessly. When the braves did spare lives they carried off their prisoners, herding them along as they moved their camps.

A relief column of troops left Fort Snelling by the end of the week. Commanded by Henry Hastings

Sibley, fourteen hundred soldiers marched through an abandoned countryside. Ruins of buildings, idle fields and uncared for animals marked the trail of the plundering Sioux.

After reaching Fort Ridgely at the end of August, Sibley began to pursue the Indians. Stopping now and then to bury scalped bodies, the soldiers ran down small bands and rescued their captives.

The Indians were in no mood to give up easily. They fought the troops at Birch Coulee, at Fort Abercrombie and finally at Wood Lake. In this last battle the Indians' resistance was broken and Sibley's troops took two thousand prisoners and released large groups of white captives.

When Little Crow realized that the Sioux uprising had failed, he urged his tribesmen to kill all their white prisoners. When the other chiefs refused he knew that his power was gone. With his kinfolk he fled into the Dakotas to seek refuge with the Plains tribes.

He left behind a fearful toll. In one month of terror he and his warriors had killed more than six hundred settlers and nearly a hundred soldiers. Thousands of frantic refugees had fled to cities and villages outside the Minnesota river valley.

Little Crow's tribesmen captured by the soldiers were tried by the Army on charges of murder. More than three hundred were sentenced to be hanged.

Public protests over the harsh sentences, particularly in the East, caused President Lincoln to review the trials. He reduced the sentences of all but thirty-nine of the worst offenders. This group was hanged on a single gallows at Mankato late in December before a great crowd of witnesses.

Little Crow remained in the West for a few months and then risked a trip back to the devastated valley, to which most of the settlers had returned. He was seen prowling around a farm near Hutchinson. The farmer ran for his gun and shot and killed the Indian chief.

CHAPTER 13

Comanche Trap

A "COMANCHE MOON" lighted the Texas plains with a bright silver sheen. The air was soft and the night invited even the oldsters out of doors. Yet no white man stirred from his darkened adobe hut. It was too risky; the brilliant moon warned of danger.

Comanche bands were abroad again, striking swiftly, killing settlers, carrying off prisoners. In the last few months the Indian raiders had become more daring. Unlike the northern plains red men, who fought the settlers only when they entered their hunting grounds, the Comanches and their Kiowa cousins rode boldly upon the settlements.

This night they attacked again. Striking terror with their eerie war whoops they surprised a little outpost on the Texas Staked Plain. With arrows and tomahawks they fell upon cowering families, butchering their victims. When they rode off they carried eleven scalps and seven white captives.

To put an end to such outrages the War Department in 1864 sent out columns of troops against the southern tribes. One force, stationed at Cimarron, New Mexico, was led by Lieutenant Colonel Christopher Carson—the famous Kit Carson, mountain man and Indian fighter. There were few craftier whites in the West.

With cavalry and infantry soldiers, Ute and Apache scouts, two howitzers and a wagon train, Carson set out in two feet of snow for Adobe Walls, in the Texas Panhandle. It was early November.

The commander planned to make the ruined trading post his headquarters. There he would leave his wagons, pack his supplies on mules and hunt for the Indian raiders.

He did not have to hunt far. Two scouts, sent ahead to find the enemies' trail, raced back to the column. "Comanches and Kiowas," the scouts reported. "Across river from Adobe Walls."

Carson at once made plans to surprise the foe. Leaving his wagon train to trail him he led his three hundred soldiers in a forced night march toward Adobe Walls.

It was still dark when they reached the old trading post. There was little cover to hide the troops as they approached the river. When dawn broke—

Suddenly a warning cry sounded from the other bank. Several Kiowas herding horses outside their village had spied the troops.

"Get your ponies!" Carson ordered his Ute and Apache scouts. "Cross the river. Stampede their horses before the Kiowas can mount them."

Stripping off their scant clothing the scouts leaped upon their ponies and dashed through the freezing water. At the same time Carson tossed aside his overcoat and led his infantry toward the river. It was still too dark to see much beyond the stream.

From the sounds of thundering hoofs and snorting horses it became clear to Carson that the Kiowa warriors were aroused and catching their mounts. Soon his scouts came crashing back across the river. Their efforts to reach the herd first had failed.

Sighting Carson's troops the Kiowas charged toward them. They clung to their horses' sides, firing from under the animals' necks.

After a quick exchange of fire the Kiowas pulled back. In the brightening dawn Carson saw another and larger village some distance away. It was a Comanche camp—in a fever of activity. Aroused by the gunfire a thousand braves were preparing to join the battle.

"Bring up the howitzers," Carson called. "Put a few shells into the Kiowa camp before that big crowd gets here."

Four shells exploded in the nearest camp, sending the warriors flying out of range. At once, Carson ordered the infantry—with the cavalry support—to cross the river. "Burn the village before the Comanches can get here," he shouted.

The troops were hardly across the stream before a

mass of braves swooped upon them, stopping their advance. Sweeping around the soldiers' flanks the Indians began to attack from the sides as well as in front.

Fighting doggedly to turn back the assault, Carson's men finally reached a position from where they could advance. Carson ordered his bugler to signal "Charge."

The troops had hardly leaped into action before another bugle call sounded. This time the order was "Retreat."

In confusion, the soldiers hesitated and looked toward Carson. He again had the bugler sound "Charge." Again "Retreat" rang out, more clearly now from the Comanches' ranks.

"Some smart chief got ahold of a bugle and is playing tricks on us," Carson said, half in admiration. "He's changing my orders. Well, forget the bugle. Let's get on with the fight."

Before they could reach the Kiowa village, Carson's force was again stopped. The commander turned the howitzers on the warriors again.

At first the cannon burst frightened the braves, but when they saw they could follow the shells' flight they merely dodged out of their way.

Finally, one shell knocked a Comanche off his pony. Several of Carson's scouts raced out to scalp the senseless brave. Before they could reach him, however, two friends of the fallen warrior galloped forward and leaned low, each grabbing an arm of the Comanche. Between them they dragged the man to safety.

Noon passed and the battle continued without letup. Indian reserves, well mounted and carrying plenty of ammunition, arrived to join the attackers. By midafternoon three thousand braves were in the fight. Each hour Carson's position became more dangerous.

Every trooper and scout knew the peril. Tired and grim, they held their fire until the more daring warriors charged in to cut down one of the enemy. His force was now trapped, Carson knew, and he must find a way to break out of it. His only hope was in retreat.

He knew he could never get back across the river without suffering terrible losses. The troops must make their way up the stream until they met their wagon train.

His orders went back to the cavalry. "Lead your horses in columns of four. Move slowly. The infantry will protect your flanks and rear. Keep fighting."

The columns began to move. The course lay across a meadow of tall bluestem grass.

The combined Kiowa and Comanche force moved quickly to plug the breach in their trap. Part of the Indian horde swept forward in a mass charge. The others set fire to the grass, sending a cloud of smoke drifting over the soldiers. Soon the men were gasping for air, half smothered by the fumes and flames leaping toward them.

"Burn the grass ahead of you," Carson shouted to his men. "Burn a trail out of the river bottom. Head for the slopes yonder."

Flames licked out ahead of the harassed column. Stopping now and then to fight off a wild charge, the troopers worked their way slowly over a hot, smoky path toward a ridge where the grass was short and scant. There they were safe from the flames that had threatened to overrun them.

Carrying their wounded on ammunition carts, Carson's force fought as they retreated. At last a cheer sounded among the cavalrymen at the head of the column.

At a gallop the wagon train tore across the sandy plain toward the soldiers. Supplies and desperately needed shells were on the way.

The Indians' hope of complete victory was now gone. The soldiers were out of their trap. Once their wagons reached them there was no chance of wiping them out. The warriors broke off the fight and the Battle of Adobe Walls was over.

"I never saw a pack of redskins fight so well or so bravely," Carson said later. "They gave us a licking."

CHAPTER 14

White Men's Shame

IT WAS summer on the plains, a season the Indians loved best. Grass was plentiful for their ponies. The buffalo were everywhere and food easy to find. Villagers roamed about at will, making their camps in cool groves beside clear streams.

In winter the tribes huddled in their tepees to escape the cold and deep snow. Game was harder to hunt. The warriors remained close to their villages, thinking only of food and shelter and how to survive until spring came.

But in summer it was different. Summer was a time of plenty, and because of this, a time for war.

In the summer of 1864 the Indians found many reasons to war on the whites. Their wagon trains and speedy stagecoaches cut deeper into their hunting grounds. The tribes were forced to move greater distances to reach the buffalo herds. Settlers were plowing the sod and planting crops. They were making their homes on Indian land.

It was a good time to strike back at the whites, the Indians knew. All the soldiers the palefaces could spare were off—fighting their brothers in the Civil

War. There were few troops in the West to protect the trails and the settlers.

In June a band of warriors moved boldly into the Denver district. They fell upon the Hulgate family on Box Elder Creek, killing the rancher, his wife and two children and stealing a large herd of cattle.

The raid threw the residents of Denver into panic. People stopped their work to hide in homes, fearful that the tribesmen would attack the city itself. John Evans, the governor of Colorado, wired an appeal to Washington to send troops for protection.

But Washington was too busy with its own troubles with the South to worry about Indian raiders in the West. The governor called for volunteer soldiers to fight the braves. Colonel J. M. Chivington was put in charge of the home guard.

Governor Evans next urged the Indians to leave the warpath. He offered them food and safety. If they would move their families to the Indian agencies near Denver, there would be no more trouble, he said.

But it was summer and such an offer of peace held no interest for the tribes. They continued their war on the whites.

Attacks upon the stages increased week by week. Guards armed with rifles and revolvers rode beside the drivers to fight warring bands. Wise passengers also carried guns to help beat off the assaults.

In August the tribes made a desperate effort to

close the trail through Nebraska. Along a stretch of three hundred and seventy miles they struck at relay stations, farms, ranches, settlers' trains, freight wagons and stagecoaches.

Barns, sheds and haystacks were burned. Homes were looted and then set afire. A family of ten was massacred and scalped at Ewbank station, where a woman was pinned to the ground by a wooden stake through her body. At Plum Creek a war party fell upon some settlers, killed nine and carried off two women and two children.

The uprising spread terror for miles on both sides of the trail. Families fled from farms and ranches, leaving behind their stock and fodder, tools, household goods and food supplies. Within a week all but one farm—from the Little Blue River to Colorado—were abandoned to the Indians. Even Julesburg, the most important home station on the route, was destroyed.

George H. Carlyle was driving his stage toward the Platte when he came upon the grisly scene at Plum Creek. After he and his passengers buried the nine mutilated bodies, they drove on. Suddenly a band of Indians appeared on a hilltop beside the trail. Whooping madly, they charged down upon the coach.

Whipping the mules, Carlyle began to race for life. Lurching and bouncing over the rough road, the passenger-filled coach rocked along while the Indians fired arrows and rifle bullets from their speeding horses. Carlyle and his guard held them off with rifle and revolver shots.

Mile after mile the race continued. Whenever the lathered mules slowed down, Carlyle whipped them for more speed. After twenty miles the Indians finally gave up the chase.

The Indians nearly drove the stagecoach line out of business. For weeks at a time not a wheel turned. When troops were sent out from Fort Leavenworth to check the marauders, the Indians attacked all the more fiercely.

The coaches able to get through began to wear out from lack of care. A passenger in one coach complained to the driver that only two boards remained in the floor and he was in danger of falling through.

"Hang onto the sides, then," the driver said and whipped up his mules.

Meals were poor and relay points were in equally bad shape. Passengers sometimes traveled thirty-six hours without food. A trip by stage was a dangerous, painful venture.

When autumn chilled the plains the red men's lust for war cooled. They thought of the food and shelter needed for the coming winter. Now the warriors were ready to talk peace.

In September Chief Black Kettle of the Cheyennes sent word to the Indian agent on the Sand Creek

Reservation that his people were willing to be friendly. To prove it he offered to give up seven white captives. He would talk peace at his camp at Bend of Timbers.

Major E. W. Wynkoop, the army commander of Fort Lyon, marched one hundred and thirty soldiers to Black Kettle's village. Not expecting such a large force the Cheyenne chief lined up six hundred warriors, ready for a battle if the whites wanted one.

"We have not come to fight," Wynkoop said. "Let us meet in council and decide what we can do."

The chiefs agreed and listened to the major's plan. "Come to Denver with me," he suggested, "and talk with Governor Evans. If your Cheyennes want peace, you will have to see the man who first offered it."

This the chiefs agreed to do and several days later met with the Colorado governor. Black Kettle and White Antelope spoke for their tribes.

"We want to hold you by the hand and have peace with the whites," Black Kettle said. "Let us take good tidings home so that our people may sleep in peace. That is all we ask."

"Months ago I called on the friendly tribes to come to the agencies," Governor Evans replied. "I have nothing new to offer you. If you want peace, you must make terms with the white war chiefs. The time is near when United States soldiers will again swarm over the plains. You can never drive the whites from the country. Give yourselves up to Major Wynkoop at Fort Lyon. You can make a peace treaty only with the army leaders."

After lecturing the chiefs for their attacks on settlers, freight and stage lines, he sent them home, promising them nothing.

As far as the chiefs were concerned the matter was settled. Although their young men were still on the warpath, the tribal heads were anxious to go into winter quarters.

Upon returning to Fort Lyon they received Major Wynkoop's permission to move their villages under the post's protection. They brought in their families, satisfied that they were again at peace with the Army. Several white prisoners were turned over to Wynkoop but their captors had mistreated them so severely they soon died. Gradually other bands came to the fort until there were about five hundred Cheyennes and Arapahoes—mostly women and children—in camp.

Governor Evans and other Colorado leaders had no thought of calling this peace. They raised two regiments of nearly one thousand volunteers for a hundred-day Indian campaign. This force enlisted to kill Indians and kill Indians they would. Their intention was backed by General S. R. Curtis, the commander at Fort Leavenworth. His message said, "I want no peace until the Indians suffer more."

The stage was set when Major Scott J. Anthony of the First Colorado Cavalry relieved Major Wynkoop as commander of Fort Lyon. Anthony ordered all Indians away from the army post. They moved their camp to Sand Creek, forty miles away.

By late November Colonel Chivington and his Colorado volunteers were ready for war. Instead of moving out on the plains where hostile bands were still raiding and killing, they marched to Fort Lyon.

The soldiers soon left the fort for the Indian villages on Sand Creek. Chivington, a huge and ruthless man, had given the orders. "Take no prisoners, kill all, big and small." The volunteers were in a mood to do just that—and they did not care whether the Cheyennes were friendly or not.

The Indian camp nestled in the bend of the stream, dry now except for scattered pools. No timber and little grass grew around the hundred lodges, ten of which belonged to the Arapahoes. The banks of the creek dropped straight down—three feet high in some places, as much as ten in others. A herd of ponies grazed across the stream from the camp. Of the five hundred Indians asleep there, about two hundred were old enough to bear arms.

The soldiers moved upon the camp at daybreak on a brisk, clear morning. The beat of horses' hoofs gave the Indians their first warning of approaching danger. Before more than a dozen tribesmen were awake bullets were ripping into the tepees. The sudden roar of gunfire threw the camp into panic.

The sudden roar of gunfire threw the camp into a panic

The attack opened near the lodges of Black Kettle and White Antelope. Unable to believe the assault was planned, Black Kettle shouted to his people to be calm and they would not be killed. To show that his camp was peaceful, the chief raised an American flag over a white flag on a pole outside his tepee.

The soldiers were dismounted now and creeping up on the doomed village. Their rifle fire thundered without letup. Half-dressed Indians leaped into the creek bed and raced to the upper end of the village, seeking protection around Chief War Bonnet. A few reached their ponies and sped off to warn camps on the Smoky Hill River.

Aware at last that the whites intended to destroy his people, Black Kettle started to run, calling to White Antelope and others to follow. White Antelope fell dead a moment later. Black Kettle, also shot, was carried off by his warriors to fight the whites another day.

Seeking refuge from the murderous fire, women and children crawled into holes along the creek's banks, believing they would be spared. Pursuing, the soldiers dragged their victims to the open. Slashing them with knives, clubbing them with gun butts or shooting them down coldly, they killed and scalped as mercilessly as the fiercest red man. It was Indian fighting at its worst. White men proved they could be as heartless and brutal as red men.

Flaming torches, whipped from one tepee to another, soon had the village ablaze from end to end. Concealed by the smoke or lost in the confusion, many Indians escaped. Only four of the Arapahoes in the camp survived.

After the slaughter the volunteer soldiers marched back to Denver carrying a hundred scalps and three cringing Indian children. For his harsh treatment of the tribesmen Colonel Chivington had an answer that satisfied the western citizen. In Black Kettle's camp his men had found fresh white scalps and parts of bodies. The soldiers were paying the red men back in their own coin. This punishment they believed necessary to force peace upon the plains.

While some people in the West accepted the "Chivington massacre" as a proper lesson for the Cheyennes, the East became inflamed by it. Newspapers, public men, even the head of Indian Affairs at Washington cried shame, even when it was proved that some braves with Black Kettle, claiming to be friendly, were just off the warpath.

The blame was never fixed. The soldiers involved were not punished because their term of enlistment was over long before they could be brought to trial.

This was only one instance where stubborn and shortsighted white men brought bloodshed and waste to a people who had no choice but to fight for their lives. Robbed of their land and denied a means of livelihood, they resisted with the only defense they knew —war to the end.

Whatever hopes the West held for peace, they were now gone. The Cheyenne and Arapahoe tribes laid their plans to make the whites pay for their betrayal at Sand Creek.

CHAPTER 15

Sioux Ambush

THE bitterness between white and red men on the central plains spread to the northern Sioux. Their best buffalo pastures lay below the Yellowstone River between the Rocky Mountains and the Black Hills—the Powder River country. By treaty the whites had pledged this area to the Sioux, Cheyennes and Arapahoes. The tribes were ready to fight anyone who dared to enter their hunting grounds.

The discovery of gold in Idaho and Montana had drawn crowds of rough and rugged miners. A wagon road was needed to haul food, tools and other freight to their camps. The best and shortest route from the East was through the Powder River country.

Once more a treaty stood in the way of the white men's interest. Army officials argued that force—and force alone—would make the red men come to terms.

The first attempt to open a road east of the Big Horn Mountains was made in the summer of 1865. General Patrick E. Connor with three thousand cavalrymen started north from Fort Laramie toward the Yellowstone River with James Bridger as their guide. Bridger, the former mountain man and friend of Oregon settlers, had little respect for the green army troops who knew little about Indians or how to fight them. "Paper collar soldiers," he called them.

Fought by the Indians most of the way, Connor was forced at last to pull back his column. His attempt to open a road to the mining camps failed.

Offers of gifts and peace were next tried to break down the Indians' resistance. Bringing a glittering array of presents, an agent of the Indian Bureau reached Fort Laramie in 1866 for a council with Chiefs Red Cloud and Man-Afraid-of-His-Horse.

The chiefs turned down the gifts and refused to make any treaty whose object was a road along the Powder River. While the council was going on, Colonel Henry B. Carrington marched into the fort from the East with a thousand infantrymen, many of them recently released from Civil War duty.

Carrington came with orders to build forts and guard a new road to Montana—the Bozeman Trail. Chief Red Cloud boldly asked the army commander where he was going.

"We are marching into the Powder River country," Carrington said.

Angrily, Red Cloud replied, "We are sent presents by the Great White Father who wants a new road through our hunting grounds. Now, before the Indians can say yes or no, the white chief comes with soldiers to steal that road. We say no. There will be war if the whites come into our country." With that, he and Man-Afraid-of-His-Horse walked from the council and rode off to the north.

"Red Cloud spoke the truth," Bridger told Carrington. "His people will fight any force they find building forts."

Anxious to heed the wise scout's warning, Carrington tried to delay his northward march but his army superiors directed him to leave at once. He drew all the ammunition he could at Fort Laramie, a mere thousand rounds for his men's muzzle-loading rifles, and set out to face thousands of hostile Indians.

By mid-July Carrington and his men reached a small plateau beside Big Piney Creek, up against the Big Horn Mountains. Here the commander planned to build Fort Phil Kearney.

Indians ran off many of the army horses almost before the soldiers made camp. Ignorant of Indian fighting methods, officers and men blundered into ambushes and several were killed and wounded in the first clashes.

Colonel W. J. Fetterman was typical of the officers with Carrington. He boasted, "Let me take fifty men and I'll ride through the whole Sioux nation."

To bring in logs and timber for a stockade and post building, Carrington sent out twenty wagons, moving in parallel columns, under heavy guard. The teamsters were ordered to form a corral at the first sign of Indians

—and prepare to fight. Should a wood train be attacked a messenger was to race back to the fort for help.

Large numbers of Indians began gathering around the Tongue and Powder rivers during the fall. An attack on the fort itself appeared to be near.

In early December, with the temperature below zero, a band of Indians fell upon a wagon train. Colonel Fetterman and a party of cavalrymen dashed out from the fort to the rescue. They found the wagons drawn up in a corral and standing off the braves.

At the sight of the cavalry the Indians fled—with Fetterman following for five miles. There the warriors turned and soon surrounded Fetterman and fourteen troopers. A group of horsemen under Carrington galloped out from the fort in time to save the colonel and his men.

In the days that followed, the Indians pestered the soldiers almost daily. No one could leave the fort except under guard. Carrington and his men were always on the defensive. This was the kind of warfare that suited the Indians perfectly. Until a large army force went out and destroyed their villages—their bases of supply—the tribes would hold the troopers at their mercy.

Unknown to the soldiers at Fort Phil Kearney, a huge party of tribesmen under Chief Red Cloud gathered in late December for an assault on the army post.

More than a thousand Arapaho, Cheyenne and Mini-conjou Sioux moved down from the Tongue River, followed by as many Oglala. They led their best war ponies, with packs of food and war clothes tied to raw-hide saddles. A few had rifles, the rest arrows and lances.

The war chiefs met in council to plan their battle. A small party was picked to attack the first wood train that left the fort. This would bring the soldiers swarming to the rescue, they knew. To lead the troops into a trap, ten decoys were named to ride toward the fort itself. Once the soldiers took after the slowly moving decoys, they would be led into the hills where hundreds of hiding Indians waited to cut them down.

The next day began as the Indians had hoped. It was December 21, 1866, and the last wood train of the season left the fort and rolled over the trail to the west. At once a small party of braves fell upon the wagons, which quickly formed a corral. At the same time the decoys rode out as though to strike at the fort.

The sound of gunfire carried into the stockade. A lookout stationed on a near-by hill signaled with flags, "Many Indians." Inside the forts, troopers ran to their horses and infantrymen grabbed their rifles. It was familiar routine by now.

Colonel Carrington voiced his warning. "Fetterman, your orders are to bring in the wood party. Do not pursue the Indians beyond the summit of Lodge

Trail Ridge." He repeated his command, then mounted a sentry platform and again cautioned the eager young officer.

The fort gates swung open and Fetterman led out his troop of bluecoats, the "pony" soldiers as the Indians called them. Behind marched a detail of infantry, known to the red men as "walk-a-heaps." There were seventy-nine officers and men—besides two civilian aids—in the relief party.

The Indian decoys were between the fort and the besieged wood train. They attracted Fetterman's attention at once and he took after them as they moved leisurely toward the hills. He forgot his orders to relieve the wood haulers.

Deep in the hills to the north lurked two thousand warriors. They had stripped the buckskin covers from their shields, painted themselves for war and sang their death songs.

Fetterman reached the top of Lodge Trail Ridge, the point he was ordered not to pass. Instead of turning back he went on, leading his cavalry and infantry down the trail to a flat at the forks of a creek. Now he and all his men were deep within the Indians' trap.

Suddenly out of the brush and from behind rocks and trees burst two masses of yelling savages, painted hideously. On horseback, they charged the surprised soldiers. They showed little fear of the whites' single-shot, muzzle-loading rifles.

At once the "walk-a-heaps" broke ranks, scrambled up the ridge and found cover among a jumble of rocks. The braves were soon upon them, shooting stone-tipped arrows, clubbing, stabbing. The blue-coated "pony" soldiers kept together, leading their horses as they fought a slow retreat up the trail.

At the top of the ridge the cavalrymen turned their mounts loose and rallied to fight. As the army horses galloped toward the fort the Indians raced after them. The battle could wait—cavalry mounts were prizes every warrior craved.

The lull lasted only a few minutes. The Indians came tearing back, charging upon the troopers from two sides. Savage hand-to-hand fighting went on as long as breath remained. The soldiers' bugler, out of bullets, battered Indian heads with his trumpet until it was flat. Forty minutes after the troopers walked into the Indians' ambush the last man went down.

On the other side of Lodge Trail Ridge the wood train fought off its attackers and moved on to safety. Inside the fort Colonel Carrington paced about nervously. What had happened to Fetterman? When he received no word from the relief party he sent out a second column and two wagons under Captain Ten Eyck.

Moving warily, Ten Eyck reached the top of the ridge. At first he saw nothing of Fetterman's command—then a cluster of naked bodies, hacked and slashed horribly.

Below him a mass of warriors danced and howled in bloody triumph. They beckoned to the relief party to come down and fight. Ten Eyck stood his ground and soon the warriors began their retreat. They could not wait to tell their villages of the great victory and begin the scalp dance. They carried away only sixteen dead.

That night a howling blizzard swept down upon the crushed soldiers who remained inside Fort Phil Kearney. Portuguese Phillips, an army scout, rode out into the storm to carry the news of the massacre to Fort Laramie, two hundred and thirty miles away. More dead than alive, he stumbled into a Christmas Eve party to stun the garrison with his fearful story.

CHAPTER 16

The Iron Horse

A CHUGGING railroad engine, white wood smoke gushing from its barrel-size stack, rumbled over the trestle at Plum Creek, in Nebraska, ahead of the private car of General Grenville M. Dodge. Picking up speed as it rocked over the new Union Pacific Railroad two hundred miles west of the Missouri River, the special train rolled toward the track's end.

A score of miles ahead, crews of men were grading down hills, filling coulees, setting out ties and spiking down rails as the roadbed crept out across the prairie. Before their work would end, the tracks would climb the long slope to the Rockies, cross the Continental Divide and join with the Central Pacific of California, which was cutting its way through the Sierra Nevada Mountains.

The two companies, one working from the East and the other from the West, were racing toward their link-up in Utah. The work was going on even while the Sioux were fighting army forces to close the Bozeman wagon trail through Wyoming.

General Dodge, called "Long Eye" by the Indians because he could see so far with his surveyor's glass,

An engine rumbled over the trestle at Plum Creek, Nebraska

was chief engineer of the Union Pacific. He was returning to oversee work being done on the railroad after a visit to headquarters at Council Bluffs, Iowa.

His car was no pleasure coach. Rifles stood in racks

along its walls. Opened cases of shells covered half the floor and cartridge belts, every loop filled, hung ready to be snapped on.

Twenty men besides the chief engineer filled a dozen seats at the forward end of the car. All of them, including "Long Eye" Dodge, were only a few months removed from the Civil War. After their release from the Army they made short visits home, then headed west for their first civilian jobs—helping to build the cross-country railroad.

From the windows the men glimpsed a buffalo herd well to the north. There were thousands more farther west, they had been told. Buffalos and Indians. The Indians were keeping out of sight, except to make quick raids on mule and horse herds or to attack groups of workmen caught away from the main camp. They were furious over the iron monsters that screamed like wildcats and drove away all the game.

The men with General Dodge were dozing in their stiff seats when their engine screeched a warning whistle and began to jerk to a stop. In surprise, Dodge stuck his head out of a window. The others did the same.

Around a bend ahead they saw a string of cars loaded with rails, kegs of spikes, bolts, sledge hammers, ties—and food for the work camp. For some reason it had halted at the head of a shallow valley.

Then the engineer of Dodge's special shouted, "Injuns! Injuns up ahead. They dragged timbers and rocks onto the tracks and stopped the freight train. They're gunning for the train crew this minute."

General Dodge withdrew his head and called, "Grab your guns, men." There was a scramble, a scraping of feet as the former soldiers dashed back for rifles. "Fall in," Dodge went on. "We're going forward and take that train from the Indians."

The men stampeded from the car as General Dodge gave another order. "Deploy on a skirmish line. Take cover in the ditches and start moving up."

The men had fought often in this manner—from Memphis to Richmond—and they needed no more orders. As soon as they crept within range they began to snipe at the warriors milling around the freight engine and shooting into the cab.

The braves returned the skirmishers' fire. When the thin line continued to advance the Indians fell back.

The episode caused no surprise to the railroad builders during the late 1860's. It was a familiar story—Indian tribes fighting stubbornly but vainly against every new advance of the white men.

To the red men the lumbering prairie schooner, the stagecoach, the pony express and now the iron horse meant the same thing—loss of hunting grounds, disappearance of the buffalo and other game, starvation, death to the villages. To make that end certain, the "pony" soldiers and the "walk-a-heaps" scattered over the plains from their forts punishing the tribes when they fought for what was once theirs without dispute.

The idea for a railway line across the West had taken hold of men's minds long before the overland mail became a reality. As early as 1850, engineers studying the western ranges had found more than one course by which a railway could cross to the Pacific. It would be a long and costly task, however. Where would the money come from?

There was another barrier, too. A northern or central route must cross the Indian frontier—lands granted to the tribes "forever." But before this, the whites had found ways to get around treaties. Was there not much land—far off from the rail routes—for the Indians?

The nation was rich and growing in the early 1850's, and it spent money freely to crisscross the East and Middlewest with railroads as far as the Missouri River. Thirty thousand miles of track were in use by 1860. The next big advance, everyone believed, would be a transcontinental line.

But the hope died when a financial panic broke in 1857. Banks closed and factories shut down. People had no use for a railroad to the Pacific then; they were worried about finding a way to live from day to day.

The hard times passed—and as business picked up old dreams returned. Even so, it became clear that the United States government would have to give rail builders a hearty boost.

Congress supplied it by offering generous payments of land. For each mile of track laid, the railroad company would receive ten sections of land along its four-hundred-foot-wide right of way. To help pay for the work, Congress voted to loan bonds to the builders, the loans varying from sixteen thousand dollars per mile on track crossing the prairies to forty-eight thousand in the mountains.

It was an offer that brought quick results. In California a company called the Central Pacific was formed in 1862 and it started its surveys at once. Actual work on the line began the next February, when ground was broken at Sacramento. A few miles of track were in use by the end of the year.

Although started with enthusiasm, the work lagged during the first five years. To cross the Sierra Nevadas the roadbed curved and twisted up canyons, across bridges and trestles, through tunnels and over high fills. It was a costly, slow task in which few people wished to risk their money. Labor was equally scarce on the West Coast and full crews were hard to find—and, once found, hard to keep.

Tools, rails, engines and freight cars had to be brought to California by sea around Cape Horn, most of them from Europe. Only a hundred and thirty-six miles of track were down by the beginning of 1868.

The job was moving still more slowly at the eastern end of the line, though the difficulties were not nearly so great. A railway from the East had reached St. Joseph in 1859, but that Missouri city was ruled out as the starting point for the push west. The government insisted that the Union Pacific begin its line at Council Bluffs, Iowa. That state had no rail connection between the Mississippi and Missouri rivers.

The first job at Council Bluffs was the building of a bridge across the Missouri to Omaha, Nebraska. Materials and rolling stock were carried by boat up from St. Louis and St. Joseph—or hauled overland by wagon. The Union Pacific had the bridge finished and forty miles of track into Nebraska by 1865, but that was all.

With the end of the Civil War, discharged soldiers from both armies took jobs on the railroads, earning a dollar or two a day and board. Ahead of the rail-laying gangs went teamsters and teams of mules, breaking the sod and grading up the roadbed. Drivers owning their own teams were paid five dollars a day. If they handled another man's mules they got two dollars, the mules three. Camps for graders housed about two hundred men and were usually twenty miles apart.

Stone and timber for bridges, rails, spikes and all the other building supplies had to be moved out from Council Bluffs. The tracks lay across unsettled plains and were menaced by Indian war parties. Everything the workmen needed—food, shelter and other supplies—was freighted out to them.

The largest group of laborers collected in the terminal town, the main camp that marked the end of the track for a few weeks. During the busy season as many as ten thousand men made up such a camp.

Usually several schemers appeared with plans to make the rail terminals permanent cities. They laid out streets, marked off lots and did their best to sell real estate. Reckless risks were taken by those eager to get rich. For weeks the buying and selling went on.

Then the order would come to "pack up and move." The crews knocked off work for the day and uprooted the camp. Boxes and bags were packed, tents pulled down, frame buildings disjointed and the whole mass piled in a jumbled heap upon freight cars and hauled off. Before sundown the camp came alive again some forty or fifty miles farther west, exactly like its former self. Behind, it left a scar on the prairie, an uncovered grave of high hopes and low life.

When the tracks reached the place that was to become Cheyenne, Wyoming, near the end of 1867, a railroad station was the first permanent building set up. The carpenters had hardly finished their work before a train rolled up with a jumble of boards, canvas, furniture and other living necessities.

A man aboard the train called to the little group watching its arrival, "Gentlemen, here's Julesburg."

What had been Julesburg, Colorado, that morning was taken off the cars and by night become Cheyenne.

CHAPTER 17

The Rail Lines Join

ALL but one item needed by the railroad workers for their daily living had to be hauled overland by freight wagon or upon the tracks already laid. That one exception was fresh meat.

The Great Plains abounded in that staple—huge herds of buffalo that grazed from the Staked Plain of Texas to the prairies of Canada.

To the railroad crews the buffalo herds offered a near-at-hand supply of roasts, steaks and stews. Veteran plainsmen, skilled with the rifle, were hired by railroad contractors to do nothing but shoot buffalo and bring in wagonloads of meat.

William F. Cody, the former pony express rider, now known as "Buffalo Bill," served for eighteen months as a railroad game killer. During this period he bagged 4,280 buffalo.

The buffalo hunter faced danger from two sources. While the Indians were the most feared, buffalo stampedes gave hunters equally close calls.

E. J. "Lucky" Baldwin once was caught in the path of a rushing herd.

A big bull led the stampede. Head down, he came

straight at Baldwin. Doing the only thing possible, Baldwin grabbed the bull's horns and threw himself upon its back.

Across the prairie raced the herd—with the hunter riding the leader. Finally the bull headed for a grove of cottonwood trees.

As he passed under a tree, Baldwin let go of the animal's horns, leaped for a branch, caught hold and pulled himself to safety. He remained in the tree until the rest of the herd dashed away.

The railroad meat hunters were not the worst plunderers of the plains. Large parties of marksmen followed the buffalo herds across their pastures, killing them by the thousands just for their hides. Before they finished their slaughter the buffalo all but vanished, while the Indians' last hope of continuing their carefree, roving mode of life was gone.

It was only natural that the Indians made war continuously upon the meat hunters and the railroad building crews. In many instances the workmen carried rifles to their jobs and stacked them beside the track before busying themselves with shovels, sledges and wrenches.

At other times a track train carried the weapons so that in case of an Indian attack a thousand men could be armed quickly. Most of them were experienced soldiers, their foremen seasoned officers. A pause to fight Indians was just part of the day's work.

During this period the Union Pacific moved its line westward at a faster pace. The more distance it spanned, the more government land and bonds it would receive.

It was high time, for the Central Pacific of California was offering a real challenge. It had solved its labor problems by bringing thousands of Chinese workmen into the United States. Now that the grading crews were breaking out of the mountains, rapid progress would be made eastward across Nevada desert country. The rival companies started a race for mileage.

The call went east for more workmen—and employment offices hired hundreds of Irishmen entering the United States as immigrants. Whole trainloads of Irish laborers went west to help build the railroad.

Crew bosses called for more speed. Where once a mile of track a day had satisfied them, they now wanted four, five, then six. To make this possible, men moved at a run, horses at a gallop.

On the heels of the rail layers came gangs of gaugers, spikers and bolters. Sledges rang as they drove spikes into ties—three strokes to a spike, ten spikes to a rail, four hundred rails to a mile.

As the building pace grew furious, a dispute arose over the exact point of meeting. The Union Pacific wanted it as far west as possible, the Central Pacific to the east. Congress finally settled the argument. In the spring of 1869 it ordered the race to end on May

10 at Promontory Point, northwest of Ogden, Utah.

As the appointed day neared, the entire nation centered its attention upon the event, awaiting word by telegraph that the rails were joined.

General Dodge, the Union Pacific's chief engineer, worked his crews through the night of May 9 to lay the final section. By noon of the tenth the last two rails were in place, ready to be spiked down.

Officers of the two railroads, with guests from both coasts, were on the scene. A telegrapher waited to tap out the word "Done" when the final spike was driven. So eager was the nation for news that operators along the line began to pester the telegrapher with questions.

"Keep quiet," he said finally. "We'll let you know when it happens." After a time he sent a message, "Hats off. Prayer is being offered."

The prayer lasted thirteen minutes and there was no message from the scene until it was over. Then the operator wired, "We have got done praying. . . . The spike is about to be presented to Sidney Dillon, president of the Union Pacific Railroad. . . . He is driving the spike. . . . DONE!"

The news flashed across the nation. A railroad, joining the Atlantic and Pacific coasts, was a reality. Of the newest span, the Union Pacific had laid down one thousand and thirty-eight miles to the junction point, the Central Pacific six hundred and thirty-eight miles.

The railroad to the Pacific—more than anything

else in the growth of the West—brought quick and lasting changes to the lives of the American people. The frontier that had divided East from West no longer stood as a wedge between them. Travel, trade and mail moved swiftly from coast to coast, making the States truly United.

At the same time, the railroad split the southern and northern plains. Never again would it be possible for wild Indians to roam at will from the Rio Grande to Canada. They would still fight for their lands but their battles would be death struggles against a stronger foe.

Within a year after the rail link-up at Promontory Point, the Kansas Pacific joined Denver to the Missouri River by rail. As towns sprang up along the tracks through Kansas and Nebraska, the evil day that the Indians feared crowded closer upon them.

CHAPTER 18

The Cowboy's West

THE dark clouds of the morning pressed lower upon the Nebraska plains. A train of freight wagons, late in starting its return to the Missouri River, lurched ahead of the north wind's stinging lash. Even before the noon corral was formed in a sheltering coulee, snow began to slant out of the Northwest.

"We're in for a nasty storm, boys," the wagon master said. "I'm afraid our rigs will be stuck right here for the winter."

By morning the train was snowbound and the men, after tying canvas covers over the wagons, prepared to mount their horses for the journey home.

"We'll just have to turn the oxen loose and let them make out the best they can," the wagon master said. "They'll be a total loss to us."

The crew rode off, abandoning the animals to the wolves and winter weather.

When travel was possible again the next spring, the wagon master started west with fresh oxen and a crew of teamsters. As expected, they found the wagons safely cached in the ravine. To their surprise, however, the animals left behind months before were grazing within a few miles of the spot. All were sleek and fat—in better condition than when turned out upon the winter plains.

"Well that beats me," one bullwhacker said. "I figured for sure those critters were done. What do you make of it?" he added, turning to the wagon master.

The boss fingered his chin for a minute. "Maybe it shouldn't be so surprising," he said finally. "There was plenty of good nourishing fodder under the snow and those oxen simply dug down to it. Buffalo have been winter grazing that way as long as a man can tell."

He frowned and looked at his crew shrewdly. "Boys, if a bunch of oxen can winter on the open range, why can't beef cattle?" he asked.

Why not, indeed! The men glanced at each other. Here was a new idea, simple yet worth millions. It would bring to the West a whole new industry. The Great Plains, from Texas to Canada, stood open and waiting for it.

For many years, the plains and chaparral thickets of Texas and New Mexico were overrun by longhorn stock, offspring of the cattle brought to America by early Spanish settlers. They were wild and vicious, worth little except for their hides.

When the United States began to expand rapidly, the growing eastern population looked beyond its local pastures for meat supplies. Texas was full of longhorns; why not bring them to eastern markets for beef?

To meet this demand, Texans gathered large herds of longhorns and drove them overland to New Orleans and St. Louis. These drives were beset with wide rivers, rustlers and hostile farmers. The latter feared the longhorns would infect their flocks with Texas fever—and to discourage the new business, armed bands often blocked the trails. Gun fights were frequent and it took tough cowboys as well as tough animals to survive the long marches.

After the Civil War, when the first railroad pushed out upon the Kansas plains, Texas cattlemen found a new approach to the eastern markets. By driving their herds northward through Oklahoma to the Kansas rail towns of Marshall, Abilene and Dodge City, the ranchers would load their stock aboard cars and ship it to slaughterhouses in Kansas City and Chicago.

Now the Texas longhorns were worth more than a few dollars for their hides. Delivered to a Kansas cow town as beef animals they brought ten to twenty dollars a head. At the end of a drive a cattleman pocketed a check for ten thousand dollars or more. The big profits drew many Texans into the business, and within a few years herds of two and three thousand animals were trailing northward.

The first favored route became known as the Chisholm Trail, named after Jesse Chisholm, a half-breed Cherokee trader and government agent. Countless hoofs dug crooked paths across the rolling prairie until the trail resembled a brown river, dusty when dry, muddy when wet. A herd might spend three months on an eight-hundred-mile drive.

This called for the close teamwork of a dozen or more skilled men. After the herd was rounded up, branded and counted on the home ranch, it marched across an unsettled region, meeting many enemies.

When under way a herd stretched out for a distance of half a mile or more. One steer, the natural leader of the flock, set the pace, walking between the right and left "point" riders, two experienced cowboys who kept the leader headed in the desired direction.

Alongside the herd rode other cowboys in the "swing" and "flank" positions, ready to turn back any animals that tried to break out of the bunch. At the end of the pack rode the "drags," two cowboys who prodded forward the slow and lagging cattle.

Immediately behind the herd came the chuck wagon carrying the crew's food and bedrolls. Riding his rolling kitchen, the cook drove two teams of mules from one camp site to the next. First up in the morning and the last to bed at night, the cook was the most important man on the drive. If good, his chuck kept the crew cheerful; if bad, it led to endless squabbles and a sour bunch of cowhands.

A wrangler with a large herd of horses, called the *remuda*, followed the chuck wagon. He had charge of the cowboys' "strings," groups of six or eight mounts

The chuck wagon carried the crew's food and bedrolls

that were the property of each rider while on the trail. The animals were trained for either day or night herding and were changed frequently to keep the cowhands freshly mounted.

The herd moved slowly, making stops at noon and

night for grazing and watering. The slow pace was important because only by giving the animals time to feed could they pick up extra weight before reaching the railroad shipping pens.

Before dark the herd was bunched on a level stretch of prairie. Night herders rode around the resting cattle —singing melancholy songs and hymns. This was designed to assure the animals that they were protected from harm.

The trail boss, usually a ranch foreman if not the herd owner, rode far ahead of the herd to scout the trail, pick camp sites and be on the lookout for trouble generally. He assigned duties to his crew and had the last word in matters of dispute.

The end of the drive brought release from the daily monotony of dirt, bad weather, the same kind of food and interrupted sleep. Once the herd was turned over to cattle buyers, or loaded aboard rail cars, the crew was ready to celebrate.

Whooping and yipping madly, a bunch of cowboys would gallop into a Kansas cow town, letting off steam by shooting out street lamps and a store window or two. Then, after a haircut and bath, they were ready to "do the town," ending their fun only when broke.

As the cattle empire expanded into Colorado, Wyoming and Montana, better strains of stock were bred. Shorthorn, Hereford and Polled Angus sires were imported and the quality of beef improved.

Of all the men who helped to develop this new western industry, Charles Goodnight ranks as the "big boss" of the range. Not only a skilled cowman and shrewd rancher, he lived by a high moral code that made him a stern enemy of liars, outlaws and cattle thieves. Through his efforts schools, courts and churches brought a softening influence upon the rough frontier.

First entering the cattle business when only twenty years old, Charles Goodnight was forced to spend much of the next ten years with troops of rangers fighting Indians. He became one of the most trusted scouts and guides in the Southwest.

After the Civil War Goodnight set up ranches in New Mexico and Colorado and also laid out the New Goodnight cattle trail to New Mexico and the Goodnight-Loving Trail to Wyoming.

He was to do his most important work in the Texas Panhandle, however. He trailed a herd of sixteen hundred cattle across three hundred miles of wilderness to the Palo Duro Canyon, where he set up a ranch two hundred and fifty miles from a railroad. A year later he went into partnership with an Irishman named John George Adair and formed the great JA Ranch—a spread of nearly a million acres grazing a hundred thousand head of cattle.

In this period the Panhandle was overrun by rustlers and outlaws. To fight the criminals Goodnight brought the stockmen together in a protective league. By helping sheriffs and courts to capture and punish cattle thieves, the group rid the Panhandle of its worst element. For forty years Goodnight carried on a ceaseless war against lawlessness.

He was always figuring out ways to make a ranch pay larger profits. He brought system to the cowboy's work, set up a plan of policing cattle trails—and by his invention of the chuck wagon he made it possible for crews to live away from ranch headquarters for weeks at a time. His methods changed life in the Texas cattle country.

A stickler for truth and fair dealing, Goodnight was among the first to support the frontier school and church. His interest in education led him to found Goodnight College, a pioneer among West Texas schools. Before he died at the age of ninety-three he was recognized as the "Father of the Texas Panhandle."

Without the cowboy the cattle empire could hardly have been possible. These loyal, hardy, carefree young men did the dangerous, grueling and tiresome work of watching over the herds as they grazed on the open range.

It was the cowboy's duty to fight off the cattle's enemies, natural or human. Storms drove herds far off their home range; the cowboy hunted them up and trailed them back. Wolves and coyotes attacked calves and the weaker animals; the cowboy ran down the killers.

The worst foes—Indians and cattle rustlers—carried guns and fought fiercely when cornered. A "shootup" was as much a part of the cowboy's job as riding line or snaking a mired steer out of a bog. For his lonely, hazardous work he was paid thirty to forty dollars a month.

His trips to town—when one was within fifty miles—were weeks apart. Silent when around strangers, shy with women, he treated both with respect. Proud and independent, he let no man belittle either himself or his horse. He would fight for no more reason than an uncivil word—neither size nor strength of an enemy frightened him.

Generous with his few belongings, the cowboy shared what he had with anyone in need. He had no great desires—the wide open spaces, the sun and wind, the hours in the saddle were the things he cherished most. He would trade jobs with no one else on earth.

The roundups—the calf hunt in spring, the beef hunt in fall—were the big events in a cowboy's life. They meant the gathering of ranch crews like his own, with hundreds of horses, scores of skilled riders, a fleet of chuck wagons. Horses were tested in half-mile races, ropers showed their skill, storytellers swapped tall tales.

When the last calf was branded the cooks reloaded their chuck wagons and moved on to the next holding ground, a day's journey away. The riders loped across the plains to repeat their work on a new section of the range. Before the roundup ended, hundreds of square miles would be searched for beef. This was excitement, good fellowship, the most fun the cowboy had all year.

The long drive, from deep in Texas to the rail towns of Kansas, gave the cowboy another change from ranch routine. In fair weather he had little to do but ride lazily beside the shuffling trail herd. On his best swimming horse he held the cattle in line as they crossed wide rivers—the Red, the Canadian, the Cimarron and the Arkansas.

When thunderstorms, hail and high winds lashed the plains and whipped the herd into a wild stampede, the cowboy galloped off to stop the mad rush, risking his life recklessly. With equal zeal he fought Indians and rustlers. He knew that if life was dull today, tomorrow probably would be far different.

The long drive widened the Texas cattlemen's knowledge of the northern plains. To deliver herds in Wyoming and Montana he traveled hundreds of miles across fresh grassland. There were no fences to confine and restrict the flocks. The free, open range offered an opportunity which many Texans were quick to seize.

CHAPTER 19

One Against Forty

THE cow town of Wichita, Kansas, was uneasy that late summer day of 1874. Trouble simmering between Manning Clements, a Texas gunman feared as a killer, and Wyatt Earp, a twenty-six-year-old deputy marshal, was coming to a boil. When they met the next time, blazing revolvers were sure to be their only greeting.

Although a newcomer to Wichita, Wyatt Earp had accepted the job of taming the noisy, gun-carrying cowhands who trailed their herds of longhorn cattle to the railroad. He told the boys where sport ended and trouble began, and he made his orders stick.

Gunmen like Manning Clements felt insulted when peace officers curbed their wild fun. After sharp words passed between Earp and the Texan, everyone knew the tilt would not stop there.

Clements did not look long for an excuse to force a showdown. He found it when Earp collected a debt owed on a piano in one of Wichita's places of entertainment. Because the piano owner was a friend of his, Manning Clements took Earp's action as a personal outrage.

Roaring angry, he promised to bring in his crew, shoot up Wichita and "tree the marshal"—force Earp into hiding until the Texans were ready to start for home.

Clements and his fifty cowhands were camped on Cowskin Creek outside of Wichita. Buckling on their six-shooters they mounted horses and set out to make their raid. A cattleman friendly to Mayor James Hope galloped ahead to warn Wichita that Clements was coming.

Quickly calling his peace officers together, Mayor Hope urged that they arm a group of citizens to stand off the angry cowboys. Wyatt Earp objected.

"Clements and his gang will come shooting if they find half the town lined up for a fight," he said, his blue eyes calm. "There'll be a lot of citizens killed before you put the Texans out of business. Everybody knows that I'm the one they're after. Since this is my fight, let me handle it my way. I want a few steady fellows to back me up and then I'll be set."

Allowed to do as he wished, Earp picked Jack Burns and Jim Cairns, two other deputies, and also eight citizens. Carrying two six-shooters and a rifle each, they headed down Douglas Avenue toward the Arkansas River toll bridge at the town's western edge. Clements and his crowd had to cross the span to enter Wichita.

A group of curious citizens began to follow the

posse to witness the coming battle. Earp stopped them and ordered the street cleared. Refusing to be denied at least a glimpse from a distance, the spectators took refuge in doorways and behind store windows.

A short block from the bridge Earp halted his posse and spaced the ten men evenly across Douglas Avenue. "Now, boys," he said, "no matter what happens, nobody opens fire until I start shooting. Even if you see me drawing my Colts, you hold off until I let loose. If that happens you can pick your own targets."

Earp could already see Clements and his gang loping across the flat on the west side of the river. Leaving his posse the deputy marshal walked ahead a dozen paces to where a pole stood at the sidewalk's edge. He drew his lean, six-foot frame behind the pole to hide himself.

Clattering onto the bridge the Texas cowboys slowed their horses to a walk. At the sight of ten riflemen blocking the street, Clements halted his men. He huddled with his leaders briefly and then the cowboys dismounted. Clements named ten of his crew to hold the horses while the rest walked on across the bridge. Afoot, they could shoot straighter and find cover easier.

Holding a revolver in each hand the Texas gunman started uptown with his pack of forty cowhands close behind. Each fingered the trigger of his six-shooter, itching for the fight to begin.

Wyatt Earp waited until the last cowhand had cleared the bridge before stepping out from behind the pole. He headed into the street at an angle, walking loose limbed and alert. His pale face tightened under the strain but his deep-set eyes never shifted from Manning Clements.

The deputy marshal's guns were still in their holsters. His hands swung over them with the rhythm of his stride, ready to drop to the butts as quick as lightning.

The sudden appearance of Earp startled the cowboys. All stopped as though on Clements' order.

"Put up your guns, Manning," Wyatt Earp said, still moving boldly toward the leader. His voice was just loud enough to carry through the cowboys' ranks.

Clements glared at the officer but said nothing. He stood as rigid as the weapons in his hands.

Earp took another step forward. "Manning, I told you to put up your guns. And that goes for the rest of your boys. Take them back to camp."

For a moment Clements waited, as though testing the deputy marshal's nerve. Then without speaking, he shoved his revolvers into their holsters, turned his back on Earp and stalked over the bridge to his waiting horse. Just as silently, his forty gunmen put up their revolvers and followed.

Earp stood in the middle of the road, not moving

until the last cowboy mounted and headed back to Clements' camp on Cowskin Creek.

Wyatt Earp, by such acts of cold courage, by his deadly shooting, by his unyielding war on outlaws, became one of the famous peace officers of America's wild West. In his game efforts to uphold the law he had the skilled help of his three brothers—Virgil, Morgan and Warren.

Together they made the name Earp one of the brightest in western legend—but the greatest was Wyatt. All were six feet tall, wiry, blue eyed and brown haired, looking so much alike that one was often mistaken for another.

Three of the Earps—Wyatt, Virgil and Morgan—teamed up with a fourth expert marksman, John H. "Doc" Holliday, in a gun battle recorded as the most famous of the West's countless shooting affairs. It took place at the O. K. Corral in Tombstone, Arizona, when that unruly mining camp was working up its reputation as "the town too tough to die."

As their fame grew, the Earps risked death daily from the many enemies their work created. Gunmen, rustlers, robbers, killers—the whole base breed of western bad men—hungered for a chance to shoot down one or more of the brothers. Such a feat would bring the slayer lasting fame.

Those who tried it, however, were never fast enough on the draw to harm Wyatt Earp. Knowing that his life depended upon shooting skill, he trained himself to act coolly and swiftly.

At the time of the O. K. Corral fight, Wyatt Earp lived in Tombstone as a United States marshal. Virgil and Morgan were there as Wyatt's deputies.

A notorious gang of rustlers and killers, headed by Ike Clanton, operated in and out of Tombstone. They were bitter in their hatred of the Earps and voiced repeated threats to shoot down the brothers. Sooner or later, law and outlaws were certain to clash.

The outlaws made no secret of their intentions. After stationing themselves at the corral, which the Earps had to pass going to or from home, they sent a messenger to the brothers.

"Tell the Earps we're ready," said Ike Clanton. "If they don't come down here to fight it out, we'll get them, one by one, whenever we see them on the street. You can also tell Wyatt that if he'll leave town we'll let his brothers alone. Otherwise, he'd better come down here and fight or we'll come after him." With Clanton that fatal day were his brother Billy, Tom and Frank McLowery and Billy Claiborne.

The three Earps stood in the midst of a crowd when Clanton's challenge reached them. Without a moment's delay they set out for the corral.

The captain of the local vigilance committee stopped them. "I have thirty-five men ready for business, Wyatt," he said. "We'll surround the corral and

They made a grim yet splendid sight

take the whole Clanton bunch. Then we'll outlaw them from Tombstone."

Wyatt Earp shook his head. "This is our job and we'll handle it without help. Much obliged anyway. Come on, boys."

Three abreast, the Earp brothers started down Fourth Street toward the O. K. Corral. Doc Holliday, carrying a shotgun as well as his much-used revolvers, ran after the Earps and insisted that he be allowed a hand in the coming row.

Wyatt tried to turn Doc back but the slender dentist, who would rather fight than fix teeth, refused stubbornly.

The Earps made a grim yet splendid sight. All wore high-heeled boots, long square-cut black coats, white shirts and string ties. Broad Stetsons shaded their bronzed faces. Handle bar mustaches made them look years older than their actual ages. Their coats were open, showing revolvers hanging low in holsters.

Without breaking step, the four swept around the corner to face the gangmen across the corral lot. Clanton had spaced his crew several feet apart, their backs to a building wall. Two cow ponies shielded the men from possible attack from the side.

The outlaws were dressed flashily in huge sombreros, silk neckerchiefs, woolen shirts, doeskin trousers, costly boots—and revolvers.

As the line of peace officers turned, Virgil Earp was first into the lot. He faced Ike Clanton. Wyatt Earp was opposite Frank McLowery and Billy Clanton, while Morgan Earp stood before Tom McLowery. Doc Holliday, at the outside of the line, was still in the road when Virgil called out to Clanton's crew, "Throw up your hands! You men are under arrest."

For answer, Frank McLowery's hand flew to the butt of his revolver. An instant later Billy Clanton,

The outlaw pitched forward

Tom McLowery and Billy Claiborne grabbed their gun handles.

Firing together, Frank McLowery and Billy Clanton opened the attack on Wyatt Earp. One bullet ripped through the marshal's coat skirt, the other tore his sleeve. Before the sound of the shots blanked out, Wyatt had his Buntline Special spurting flame. A slug from his revolver plowed into Frank McLowery's stomach, pitching him forward.

Tom McLowery leaped behind one of the horses beside him. Firing from under the animal's neck he cut a hole in Morgan Earp's coat. By that time Billy Clanton had fired three times at Wyatt, missing each time. Morgan fired his gun at Billy, a bullet hitting him in the hand.

Ignoring Billy Clanton's fire, Wyatt turned on Tom McLowery as the most dangerous gunman, now that his brother Frank was down. Tom was still protected by the horse and a slug from his revolver caught Morgan Earp in the shoulder.

To force Tom into the open, Wyatt Earp aimed at the horse. He shot into the animal's withers. It dashed for the street, taking the other horse with it.

Meantime, Billy Claiborne was firing at Virgil Earp. After missing three times, Billy raced across the corral lot toward the open door of an adjoining building. Seeing Claiborne run, Ike Clanton, the boastful gang leader who had not yet drawn his revolver, took after Billy in a panic to reach shelter.

Now Tom McLowery fired again, sending a second bullet into Morgan Earp. Immediately Wyatt fired at Tom but it was Doc Holliday's shotgun blast that tore into Tom's stomach and sent him reeling to his death.

Gunfire was continuous now. Virgil Earp broke Billy Clanton's gun arm with his first shot. Frank McLowery, although desperately wounded, fired at Wyatt and missed. Crash of glass warned the peace officers of danger from another direction. Billy Claiborne was shooting from the building sheltering him and Ike Clanton.

Doc Holliday silenced Claiborne's fire with two revolver shots. Then Ike broke from the building and ran toward the corral stalls, throwing aside his loaded revolver. Doc fired at Ike twice, missing both times.

Frank McLowery and Morgan Earp, both suffering from gun wounds, fired at each other at the same instant, Frank falling with a bullet through his head.

Wyatt Earp, with Tom McLowery out of the way,

swung on Billy Clanton and shot him in the hip. An instant later Virgil's bullet creased Clanton's scalp.

Gamely, the outlaw forced himself to sit up. He tried to rest his revolver upon his knee for a last shot. Seeing that Billy Clanton was desperately hurt, Wyatt and Virgil withheld their fire. Then, abruptly, Billy toppled over into the dust and the battle was finished.

Not more than thirty seconds had passed beween the first and last shots in the bloody fight. The dead were Frank and Tom McLowery and Billy Clanton—outlaws all. Virgil Earp's leg wound and Morgan Earp's shoulder injury were not serious. Doc Holliday was only scratched.

After the battle Ike Clanton and Billy Claiborne were found in hiding a little distance from the corral. Jailed, they were put under guard to prevent lynching or escape. Ike, the leader, not only went willingly—he begged for protection.

Six thousand dollars in currency was found on the dead outlaws. Ike Clanton and Billy Claiborne carried large sums also. From this it was believed that the outlaws intended to flee into Mexico after killing the Earps.

CHAPTER 20

The Sioux Are Crushed

WHILE cowboys, gunmen and peace officers were giving the West a new flavor, the Indian problem was far from settled. White men and red men could not live together, it had been proved. Only by setting aside definite areas for the tribes was there hope of having peace on the plains.

The white men wanted the southern Indians to settle in Indian Territory—now Oklahoma—and the northern bands in Dakota. Thus they would be well away from the areas the white men planned to develop.

To reach an understanding with the Sioux and Cheyennes, another council was called at Fort Laramie. The leaders of the northern tribes refused even to talk peace until the United States Army had withdrawn its soldiers from the forts in Wyoming and given up the Bozeman Trail to Montana.

When these terms were met, Chiefs Red Cloud, Sitting Bull and Crazy Horse were satisfied. They signed the treaty without realizing they had promised that their tribesmen would settle down as farmers and keep hands off the railroads and wagon trails outside their reservation.

The East now believed that the Sioux and Cheyennes had given up the Powder River country. This the Indians did not intend to do.

When they understood fully the terms of the Fort Laramie treaty they were wildly angry. They would never become farmers nor let strangers—red or white—upon their hunting grounds. The white man's word meant nothing to them any more.

They became bitter at Indian agents who, they claimed, cheated them. Rations they bought were shoddy and short of weight. Their anger led them to war on neighboring tribes.

Army troops at Fort Lincoln in Dakota territory were joined about this time by General George A. Custer, a Civil War officer commanding the Seventh Cavalry.

In 1874 General Custer headed a large company of soldiers and civilians on a mission to blaze a wagon road through the Black Hills, a mountainous region full of game and sacred to the Sioux.

Custer was carrying out orders that violated treaty agreements made with the Indians. The white men had given their word that they would keep out of the Black Hills.

Little might have come of Custer's travels had not his column stopped beside French Creek, near the southern slopes of the hills. But while camped there, an engineer with Custer discovered gold.

Gold! It was the magic word that set white men's blood on fire. After that nothing—neither treaties nor guns nor scalping knives—could keep the white men out of the Sioux's last hunting paradise.

When the first gold hunters appeared, the red men protested and then fought back. The gold rush grew in volume and frenzy. By the summer of 1875 a thousand miners were in the hills.

"Open the Dakotas to the white men," the nation demanded of Congress. Hoping to make peace with the Sioux a delegation went west in September to meet Chiefs Red Cloud and Spotted Tail. They offered the tribes six million dollars for the Black Hills. The Indians not only refused to sell but threatened to kill the peacemakers, who were lucky to escape with their lives.

Now all public sympathy for the Indians vanished. More gold hunters poured into the hills. In December the tribes were given two months to get back to their reservations and stay there—or be punished.

The winter was bitter and many Indian villages were hundreds of miles from the reservation. Besides, the red men were sullen. The deadline passed and none reached the agencies. The United States declared war on Sitting Bull and his people.

Knowing that when spring came the scattered tribes

would be harder to catch, the Army planned a winter campaign. March arrived before General George Crook, another famous Indian fighter, was ready to lead his troops northward from Fort Fetterman to attack the warriors in the Powder River country.

While looking for Crazy Horse's band, a detail under Colonel J. J. Reynolds bungled its attack on an Indian village and most of the tribesmen escaped.

Now the War Department planned a summer campaign to do the job. It ordered out three columns of troops—one from Montana, another from Dakota and the third from southern Wyoming. They were to close in on the tribes at the northern end of the Big Horn Mountains, destroy their villages and horses and take them prisoners.

General Crook again led the column from the south. Leaving Fort Fetterman in late May, he reached the Rosebud River to find a thousand warriors under Crazy Horse blocking his path. A savage fight took place, forcing Crook to pull back to his wagon base on Goose Creek.

Meantime, General Alfred Terry was marching toward the Rosebud from Dakota. With him was General Custer and his famous cavalry. While riding in advance of Terry's column Custer struck Sitting Bull's trail.

Although under orders to go no farther than the mouth of the Rosebud, Custer saw a chance to whip

Sitting Bull singlehandedly. His fame as an Indian fighter would reach a new height. He might even be elected President of the United States.

Scouts warned Custer of a huge hostile camp on the Little Big Horn River. The general expected the red men to flee at the sight of him. He never dreamed that his seven hundred men and officers would face nearly six thousand seasoned Sioux and Cheyenne warriors. He was eager to fight—and since hostile scouts had discovered his approach he had to act quickly.

Dividing his force into four groups, Custer led five troops of cavalry into battle. The others were to hit the Indian camp from different sides.

It was a gallant but reckless plan that could only fail. The first detachment to meet the tribesmen was quickly beaten back. It fell across the river and was pinned down on the heights beyond.

Driving in from the east, Custer soon found himself overwhelmed between waves of yelling braves thirsty for revenge. Calmly and stubbornly the golden-haired general and all his troops fought to the death. When the battle ended on June 25, 1876, Custer and two hundred and sixty-four men of the Seventh Cavalry lay hacked and slashed on the bloody slopes of the Little Big Horn.

There Custer made his last stand. Despite their victory over a hated enemy, the Sioux and Cheyenne had done themselves more harm than good. For now

There Custer made his last stand

a nation, shocked by this latest massacre, clamored for enough troops to crush the hostile tribes.

Refusing to surrender, the Indians fought back hopelessly. Pressed by ever larger armed forces, Sitting Bull fled to Canada to find refuge for a short time. Other chiefs were forced to sign away the tribes' rights to the Black Hills. In desperation a few holdouts resisted, only to have their villages destroyed and their women and children shot down. One by one the crushed and humbled leaders were brought to the agencies, prisoners of the white men.

When white men first came to America there were about three hundred thousand Indians living in what is now the United States. They hunted wild game for food and pitched their tepees wherever they wished. A free, wild life satisfied them completely.

The white men had other customs and methods. They farmed the land, raised cattle, built roads and cities. Factories, stores and great industries made them rich and powerful.

The red men's way of life was totally different from that of the white men. When their interests clashed, war resulted. The Indians suffered many wrongs. They were cheated, robbed, abused and shown little mercy —and less justice—by the invaders of their country. The treaties they signed were broken; promises made to them were not kept.

It is a shameful record of which the people of the

United States cannot be proud. Happily, the nation is now making efforts to help the new generations of American Indians.

In other books you may read more about how the Indians and those who invaded their lands settled their differences. It is not a pleasant story, even though all rights and wrongs were not on one side.

Strife, struggle and danger were the elements of life in that period.

CHAPTER 21

"Stick 'em Up"

THE outlaw was as much a product of the wild West as was the mountain man, bullwhacker, cowboy, peace officer and the Indian himself. Wherever wealth appeared in any form the bad man followed.

As soon as stagecoaches crossed the plains they became targets of robber gangs. When they branched out to the gold fields and took aboard small fortunes in dust and nuggets, the stages were forced to carry guards for their protection.

But the highwaymen were hard to discourage. Coaches were held up so often on some trails that the mules stopped out of habit at certain spots favored by the robbers. It was a distressing state of affairs until one shipper hit upon the plan of keeping live rattlesnakes in the express box with his gold.

A silver mine owner foiled the bandits by melting his bullion into cannon balls. These seven-hundred-and-fifty-pound lumps baffled the bandits and they sent word to the man that he was not playing fair with them.

The end of the Civil War boosted the outlaw ranks.

The rabble among the discharged soldiers headed west and made crime their trade. Every stampede brought in a quota of men who would rather steal than dig gold.

Women were not barred from the outlaw's game. Dutch Kate, one of California's rougher natives, stopped a stage and ordered the driver to toss out the strongbox. It contained little—and she rode off, grumbling. She missed fifteen thousand dollars a passenger carried in a suitcase!

Another female road agent seized in the act of holding up an Arizona stage went on trial before twelve gallant jurors. They freed her of the robbery charge but sent her to jail because she had disarmed the coach driver—a very unladylike act.

The holdup trade became big business when road agents entered the Black Hills in the 1870's. The rich Homestake mine sent shipments of gold—sometimes as much as two hundred thousand dollars—by stage express from Deadwood, South Dakota, to the railroad at Sidney, Nebraska.

A special coach, built with rifle slots through its armor plate, was brought in for the job. Old Ironsides, as the rig was called, was protected by two armed horsemen riding in front, two at the rear and four other messengers inside and on top.

Some early outlaws specialized in raids on railroad trains and banks. Perhaps the most notorious of these were Jesse and Frank James, who began their careers to "get even" for attacks made on their Missouri home during Civil War days.

As other outlaws did, the James brothers claimed they were driven to crime. To them the railroads and banks were to blame for the troubles of many poor people. To get revenge the brothers turned to robbery, continuing their lawbreaking for fifteen years.

Many people felt as the James boys did and gave them food and shelter while they hid from police. Their friends and well-wishers made it possible for them to escape arrest for years.

Jesse James was hardly the picture of a typical bad man. His narrow face wore a disarming smile and his nose was small and turned up. When he wanted a disguise he grew dark-brown whiskers. He liked to dress well and usually appeared in a brown suit, white shirt and gloves, the latter to hide a finger tip shot off in a gun battle. His hands were almost as small as a woman's.

The James brothers had three partners in crime. Their cousins—Robert, Coleman and James Younger—added fearlessness to the Jameses' cunning and vengeful natures. The Youngers accepted Jesse as their leader and backed him in every enterprise, no matter how daring.

Although their holdups and robberies were usually of a rash nature, the James gang sometimes made them look like fun, especially if it concealed their crooked purpose. Their method of looting a bank at Croydon, Missouri, had the stamp of a practical joke.

The James boys, with the Younger brothers and two more aids, rode into Croydon, each carrying a potato sack across his saddle. They were dressed like farmers coming to town for groceries.

It was a special day at Croydon. A large crowd packed the courthouse commons to hear candidates make election speeches. It was the biggest show in town.

The seven young riders circled the crowd without drawing any attention to themselves. They went quietly to the bank where three of them dismounted and went inside. The others stood watch in front. Their caution was hardly needed because everyone but the cashier was over listening to the political speakers.

The trio inside the bank threatened the cashier with revolvers, bound and gagged him and remarked that it was a lovely day for their visit. Then they stuffed forty thousand dollars in bank notes into their potato sacks and rejoined their companions.

Instead of riding out of town at once, Jesse James suggested to his pals that they stop by the courthouse to hear the oratory. They sat quietly at the edge of the crowd until finally Jesse called to the speaker for attention. Although irked by the interruption, the candidate asked Jesse what he wanted.

"I just thought you might like to know some fellows tied up the cashier at the bank," Jesse said. "Maybe somebody ought to go over and untie him. I can't myself, I got to be going."

He rode off slowly, followed by his six companions clasping sacks bulging with loot. The citizens thought that Jesse was a heckler having his little joke, but at last someone did stop at the bank to look in. By then the James-Younger gang was on its way to a hide-out.

Jesse's warped humor took unexpected turns. Once he and his gang called at a farmhouse for a meal. As they ate they learned from the farm woman that she was about to lose her land because of an unpaid fourteen-hundred-dollar mortgage.

"When do you need the money?" Jesse asked.

"Today," the woman said. "A collector will be here soon and I cannot meet the debt."

To her amazement Jesse reached into a potato sack beside him, pulled out a fistful of bills and gave her enough to cover the mortgage. The bandits then waited near the farm until the collector called. After he left they held him up and took back the same fourteen hundred dollars.

For ten years the James-Younger gang robbed as they willed—and then it made a famous raid on the First National Bank of Northfield, Minnesota. It took place on September 7, 1876.

In typical James style the outlaws started their day's task quietly. Five strange horsemen rode into Northfield about noon and stopped at a restaurant. Their linen dusters implied that they were merely passing through town on a long trip.

After an unhurried meal the men remounted and rode across the Cannon River bridge. Three of them tied their horses in front of the bank, strolled to the corner and sunned themselves on some dry goods boxes on the sidewalk. Had the passing citizens known that the three were Jesse James, Bob Younger and Charles Pitts they would have paid closer attention.

Presently their two companions rode up the street and also stopped in front of the bank. With hardly a glance at the two—Coleman Younger and Clel Miller—Jesse, Bob and Charlie walked into the bank and went about their business.

A minute later a hardware merchant came around the corner to deposit some money. He was stopped by Miller but not before he saw what was going on. Jerking out of the bandit's grasp the merchant ran toward his store and shouted, "Boys, they're robbing the bank! Get your guns."

With the alarm sounded, the two lookouts jumped upon their horses and raced up and down the street, yelling madly and shooting at anyone who dared to step outside. Suddenly three more horsemen—Frank James, Jim Younger and William Stiles—joined the two guards, firing through windows and forcing the townspeople to take cover.

Inside the bank the three robbers were trying to make the cashier, a teller and a bookkeeper open the safe. All refused, claiming it was closed by a time lock—a bit of fiction that saved the bank's funds. One robber struck the cashier over the head with his revolver; another shot the teller in the shoulder as he ran out the back door.

By now the street was in an uproar. Horses dashed up and down, their riders firing as fast as they could reload their guns. One citizen dropped with a bullet through his heart. Grabbing up shotguns and rifles handed out by the hardware merchant, the townsmen rushed back to answer the deadly challenge.

Unable to find any money, Jesse James, Bob Younger and Charles Pitts fled from the bank. One bandit shot the cashier and then ran to his horse.

For once the James boys and their cousins had started something they could not finish. Blasts of gunfire toppled Clel Miller and Bill Stiles dead in the street. The other outlaws, two badly wounded, sped away on their horses. The bloody raid was over in seven minutes.

When the alarm spread throughout southern Minnesota a thousand farmers and Northfield residents joined in the bandit hunt. Two weeks passed before a posse cornered the Younger brothers and Charlie

By now the street was in an uproar

Pitts. In the gun fight that followed, Pitts was killed and Bob, Jim and Coleman Younger were wounded. The brothers paid for their life of crime by serving long terms in the Minnesota State Prison.

Jesse and Frank James were the only Northfield raiders who escaped. While being chased, they dived off a cliff into a lake, hiding in dense foliage until it was safe to move. In time they reached a Missouri hide-out.

After their disaster in Minnesota the James boys became bank shy. Three years later they formed another outlaw band that robbed three trains. By then, however, sentiment toward the outlaws had changed—and after several arrests and killings, the gang was curbed.

Jesse became a marked man. A reward of ten thousand dollars was offered for his capture.

Early in April, 1882, he took refuge with his wife and two children in a house in St. Joseph, Missouri. Charles and Robert Ford, two of Jesse's aids in crime, moved in with the family. They plotted secretly to kill their leader and collect the reward.

But they could never catch Jesse without his revolvers in his belt until one hot day he put them aside to work in the house. As he reached up to dust a picture on a wall, he was surprised by the Ford brothers. Both drew revolvers. Robert fired first, his shot entering the back of Jesse's head, killing him instantly.

The slayer collected only a hundred dollars of the reward but he ended the James brothers' career. Frank James gave himself up six months later. Tried twice for his crimes, he was found not guilty and led an honest life thereafter.

CHAPTER 22

Bad Men and Gun Fighters

NOT all bandit gangs start out as enemies of society. Three Dalton brothers—Emmett, Grattan and Robert—became holdup men and robbers after they had served as United States deputy marshals and police officers in Oklahoma territory.

Starting their evil ways as horse thieves in Kansas, they soon turned to train robbery. On their way to California the brothers looted an express car at Alila. In the chase that followed, Grattan was captured but managed to escape. Thereafter, the Daltons returned to their home range and made off with thousands of dollars by robbing trains at Wharton and Red Rock. In these raids they were helped by three other outlaws.

The Dalton gang perfected a daring but effective system for holding up trains. They divided the job into three details, assigning two men to each task.

The first called for a pair to mount the engine cab, force the engineer to stop the train and the fireman to put out his boiler. Another pair of robbers entered the coaches and held passengers and train crew at gun point while they emptied their pockets.

Most important and more dangerous was the attack

upon the express car, usually protected by shotgun guards. Battles between robbers and expressmen were sometimes to the death.

When planning a train robbery the Dalton band cast lots to decide what each member would do. In this way each took a chance on drawing the most perilous job.

Vain as well as desperate, the Daltons planned a bold act that would outdo anything the James boys attempted. They hit upon the idea of robbing two Coffeyville, Kansas, banks at once. Thus they would not only create a sensation but bag enough loot to make them all rich.

Like the James gang, however, the Daltons overreached themselves. The citizens of Coffeyville met the bandits in a roaring gun battle. The gang killed four townspeople but lost four of their own number —Robert and Grattan Dalton and two aids.

Although wounded, Emmett Dalton could have escaped but he turned back to help his brother Grattan and was captured. He served a long prison term, after which he reformed and became a law-abiding citizen.

The Daltons packed their crime into two violent years in which they stole one hundred and sixty-nine thousand dollars from trains, express offices and banks. Their loot brought death to two of the brothers and prison to the third.

One of the most famous train and stagecoach robbers that the West produced was Sam Bass, who was a deputy sheriff before striking out for "easy money." After a try at horse stealing he went to the Black Hills to rob coaches carrying gold from Deadwood.

With five other bandits, Bass made the biggest "strike" in 1877. The gang held up a train at Big Springs, Nebraska, robbing the express car of sixty thousand dollars in gold and the passengers of another five thousand. Chased by law officers three of the outlaws were slain.

Bass, always free with his money, soon needed more—and he formed another band that held up four trains in Texas. One of his own men betrayed him to the Texas Rangers, who set a trap and killed him.

Sam Bass was a desperado of the type who feared nothing but mob violence and the rope. His only reward for a life of violence was a short span—twenty-seven years. His epitaph reads: A BRAVE MAN REPOSES IN DEATH HERE. WHY WAS HE NOT TRUE?

Billy the Kid, rarely called by his real name, William H. Bonney, became the most famous outlaw of the Southwest. Although born in New York City, he was taken to Kansas when young and exposed to the evils of frontier life. Saloons became his playground—and at the age of twelve he had taken his first life. When Billy was shot to death by Sheriff Pat Garrett when twenty-one, he had killed a man for every year of his life.

A leading figure in the war among southwestern cattlemen, Billy killed in cold blood. Small and slender, he became an expert gunman, his left hand flashing to his holster with the speed of a striking snake. Anyone who got in the way of his cattle thefts was shot down mercilessly.

He once escaped from jail, where he was being held to await hanging, by killing two guards—even though shackled with leg irons and handcuffs. The dapper little desperado was trapped in a New Mexican home and shot before he could fulfill his wish to slay two more men on his list of enemies.

Billy the Kid's life again proved the old truth about the poverty of crime.

As cruel as Billy became, his base record fell far short of the bloody mark blazed by John Wesley Hardin, Texas' worst bad man. Hardin had killed six men in gun fights before he was sixteen years old. He had raised the number to fifteen two years later and to thirty-five by his twenty-fifth birthday.

A man with a fiery temper, he was the kind of killer who would shoot a buffalo hunter on a Wichita street for wearing a silk hat. After he had chalked up forty-three slayings, he served a long prison term and later practiced law. But he died from a gunman's bullet through his head.

Wild *Bill Hickok* was attacked by three outlaws

In all, two hundred and fifty bad men darkened the records of America's wild West. Against that vicious crowd stood a handful of courageous sheriffs, deputies and marshals, the gun fighters feared and hated by every outlaw.

In this group of peace officers were men like the Earp brothers, William "Bat" Masterson, William M. Tilghman, Patrick Sughrue, Charles Bassett and Captain John R. Hughes. They upheld the law and made it triumph during a period when violence threatened to rule the West.

But best known of all the men on the side of law and order was James Butler Hickok, the "prince of the pistoleers." Hickok, who wrote his name large in western legend as Wild Bill, became a famous peace officer, soldier, hunter and scout because of his uncanny skill with firearms.

As a Union spy in the Civil War he was caught more than once and sentenced to be shot, but by his quick wit and lightning actions he escaped from his captors. When a marshal at Hays City, Kansas, then the wildest town on the frontier, he was attacked by three men, all of whom he killed. The number of thieves and gunmen he shot is in dispute, but they were many.

A handsome, quiet-mannered man, there was nothing about him to suggest the border bully. Yet he always had to be on guard because of the gunmen waiting for a chance to shoot him down.

One of Wild Bill's favorite tricks was to drive a cork through the neck of a bottle with a pistol shot at twenty paces. In another, he would shoot at a dime and split the bullet on the coin's edge.

Once he appeared in Kansas City's Market Square with a new set of ivory-handled revolvers. Asked what he could do with the flashy weapons at a distance, he suddenly whipped out one gun and fired five shots at a target a hundred yards away. Snapping up the other revolver, he as quickly emptied it at the same target.

"Now someone take a look at the first letter O in that saloon sign across the square," Bill suggested. Examination of the sign showed that all ten of Bill's bullets were inside the letter.

Wherever there were crowds and excitement Wild Bill was sure to appear. The gold rush to the Black Hills brought him to Deadwood in 1876.

Deadwood by then was a seething, wicked, lawless camp of twenty-five thousand miners and riffraff. Its stores, saloons, tents and shanties staggered along the gulch floor and clung to the cliffsides. Through the camp moved mobs of miners, scores of horsemen and soldiers, freight wagons and stagecoaches.

Everyone packed a six-shooter along with his bag of gold dust. Shootings were a routine part of Deadwood's life, almost as much as its gambling and drinking.

To Deadwood came the veteran miners of all the

West and the notorious characters it bred. Among them was Calamity Jane, the strangest woman on the frontier.

Her correct name, Martha Canary, was unknown to the rough and boisterous people with whom she associated. Garbed in men's clothing and wearing her hair short, she looked as much like a man as the men around her. For years she drove mules and oxen on the plains, scouted for the Army and fought Indians —or any other enemy—with the daring of the boldest frontiersman.

The law had little force in Deadwood when Wild Bill arrived, but his reputation threw fear into the outlaw ranks. Believing the nerveless gun fighter had come to break their rule of the camp, the gangsters hired Jack McCall, a swaggering bad man, to murder Hickok.

McCall watched Wild Bill's movements for a time. At last, on August 2, 1876, McCall found his victim seated at a card game, his back to the door. Moving to within a few feet of the players, the outlaw pulled his revolver and fired into Bill's head, killing him outright.

McCall was caught and tried for murder, but his friends were on the jury and they freed him. He fled from Deadwood but was captured later and forced to stand trial in a legal court. This time he was convicted and hanged.

The murderer, robber and thief appeared upon the western scene soon after gold was discovered in California. He prowled the gold fields as long as there was color to tempt him.

The true bad man of the West grew up with the cattle ranches and cow towns. He was a lone wolf, suspicious of everyone and fast on the draw.

With the advance of the railroads and the growth of cities, the train robber and bank bandit had his day. No matter what his field, the western criminal in the end had to reckon with the law—and the law triumphed.

CHAPTER 23

They Tamed the West

ONCE the Indians were crushed and the buffalo reduced to small roving herds, the Great Plains lay open to the ranchers and cattlemen. Until 1885 the trails were packed with steers moving northward. The grassland, extending into Canada, became crowded with cattle always on the search for more pasture.

To make room for their growing droves the cattlemen shipped hundreds of thousands of head each fall to Kansas City and Chicago. As the supply increased, the packers cut their prices, paying whatever they chose. The growers' profits fell off alarmingly.

A new invention—barbed-wire fencing—came to the ranchers' rescue briefly. Now they could enclose their ranges and—without the expense of large crews of cowboys—hold their herds close to headquarters.

When the packers' prices were too low the rancher refused to ship his beef. He could afford to keep his stock for another year upon his fenced-in land—usually government land which he leased for a small fee.

The railroads, by moving out upon the plains to link up with the cattle trails, had made the cow country possible. In the 1880's they helped to destroy it.

The rich grasslands were ideal for a different type of agriculture—farming and especially the growing of wheat. No longer was it necessary to go west by covered wagon. Since the railroads offered a quick, cheap means of reaching the prairies, farm families by the hundreds flocked into the Plains States.

Settling on homesteads staked out of government land, the farmers cut the cattlemen's range. Their fences barred stock from streams and water holes. Bitterness between ranchers and farmers resulted in many clashes, often ending in gun fights.

But the tide was too great for the cattlemen to check. Their remaining land became overstocked and the grass disappeared. Their ranges were pushed farther west—to the dry uplands and mountain areas beyond the grainfields of Kansas and Nebraska.

As the region became settled, villages and towns took root, many to thrive later as busy and wealthy cities. The homesteaders and ranchers built a solid base on which grew the West as we know it today.

It is a region developed beyond any dream of the mountain men, the Forty-niners and the pioneers on their way to Oregon. The mountains and high plains grow more cattle and sheep than ever grazed on the level grasslands. Dry areas which the pioneers scorned as "desert" are now watered by irrigation and grow cotton, grain, alfalfa and fruit.

Great dams hold back the mountain rivers and pro-

Dry areas are now watered by irrigation

duce electricity for industries of many kinds. Immense harvests of wheat and corn come from the soil that gave the first settlers a bare living.

Railroads and smooth highways reach the far corners where covered wagons and stagecoaches never ventured. While airplanes now fly over the mountains in hours, the first settlers toiled weeks to conquer them —many dying in the attempt.

The explorers and trappers passed over hills and through valleys that rested upon lakes and pools of hidden oil—the fuel that now drives our automobiles. The western ranges are giving up copper, silver and coal that are worth many times all the gold dug in the days of the westward stampedes.

Every state west of the Mississippi has its natural beauties—parks, canyons, caves, mountain peaks and waters—that attract millions of visitors yearly.

The pioneers received a meager reward for the risks and hardships they endured to open a wilderness. But in return they gave generously of a quality that cannot be measured in wealth. The courage and spirit of the men and women of the frontier have become our national heritage.

That pioneer spirit is still at work in the West. Although no longer wild, the West is still young and full of vigor, building ever bigger and better, making today a steppingstone for a greater tomorrow.